EXTRAORDINARY RECIPES FROM

HOUSTON CHEF'S TABLE

ARTHUR MEYER

Photography by Terry Vine

THE BAYOU CITY'S ICONIC RESTAURANTS

Globe
Pequot

Guilford, Connecticut

The culinary community is always growing and changing. Chefs move on, while restaurants come and go. This book celebrates the chefs and dishes that have given each city or region its unique flavor. We hope you will try these recipes at home and allow their legacy to live on for years to come.

Globe Pequot

An imprint of The Rowman & Littlefield Publishing Group, Inc.
4501 Forbes Blvd., Ste. 200
Lanham, MD 20706
www.rowman.com

Distributed by NATIONAL BOOK NETWORK

Copyright © 2012 by The Rowman & Littlefield Publishing Group, Inc.
First Globe Pequot paperback edition 2020

All interior photos by Terry Vine unless otherwise noted.
Photos by Terry Vine; author photo courtesy of Arthur Meyer
Spot art on pp. 31, 57, 60, 78, 127, 147 licensed by Shutterstock.com
Map by John Wilson

British Library Cataloguing in Publication Information available

Library of Congress Cataloging-in-Publication Data available

ISBN 978-1-4930-4709-3 (paperback)
ISBN 978-0-7627-9093-7 (e-book)

∞™ The paper used in this publication meets the minimum requirements of American National Standard for Information Sciences—Permanence of Paper for Printed Library Materials, ANSI/NISO Z39.48-1992

This book is dedicated to
all who work in the Houston food service industry.

CONTENTS

ACKNOWLEDGMENTS. ix

INTRODUCTION xi

BACKSTREET CAFE 1

BARBED ROSE 5

benjy's UPPER WASHINGTON 8

BISTRO ALEX 10

BISTRO PROVENCE 14

BRANCH WATER TAVERN 18

BRASSERIE 19 20

CANOPY 26

CIAO BELLO 31

CINQ 34

DAMIAN'S CUCINA ITALIANA. 38

D'AMICO'S ITALIAN MARKET CAFE. 42

GIGI'S ASIAN BISTRO AND DUMPLING BAR 45

HAVEN 52

HUBBELL AND HUDSON BISTRO 56

Hugo's 60

Huynh 64

Ibiza Food and Wine Bar 72

Indika 76

Kata Robata 78

Latin Bites Cafe 82

Line and Lariat 86

Mai's Restaurant 90

Mark's American Cuisine 92

Max's Wine Dive...................................... 96

Mockingbird Bistro 99

Molina's Cantina 102

Monarch.. 105

Nino's / Vincent's / Grappino di Nino.......... 108

Ooh La La Dessert Boutique 113

Original Ninfa's on Navigation 116

Ouisie's Table 120

Philippe Restaurant and Lounge 123

Pondicheri 127

Prego 130

Quattro 132

RDG and Bar Annie 134

Samba Grille 138

Shade 144

Soma Sushi 147

Sparrow Cookshop & Bar 150

Tasting Room 153

III Forks 156

Tony Mandola's 158

Tony's 162

Trevisio 166

Uchi 169

Valentino's 176

Zimm's Little Deck 180

Index 184

About the Author 188

Acknowledgments

A project with a scope as vast as this could not have been done without the cooperation of so many kind and generous people. I'd like to thank the following and apologize for leaving anyone out.

Greg Morago, of the *Houston Chronicle*, who led me in the right direction at the beginning of the project.

The following agents and communications specialists who arranged for meetings, tastings, and coordinated retrieval of recipes: Mark Sullivan of On the Mark Communications, Geralyn Delaney Graham of Resources Communications, Stuart Rosenberg of Studio Communications, Paula Murphy of Patterson & Murphy Public Relations, Kimberly Park of Kimberly Park Communications, Mark Hanna of Customer First, and Michelle LeBlanc of Blue Sky Marketing.

And their assistants: Katherine Orellana, Lauren Levicki, Katy Mayell, Irena Hixxon, and Cristina Terrill.

The following owners and restaurateurs for taking time out of their hectic schedules to talk with me: Tony Vallone of Tony's and Ciao Bello, Tony and Phyllis Mandola of Tony Mandola's, Steve Zimmerman of CINQ and Zimm's Little Deck, Vincent Mandola of Nino's/ Vincent's/Grappino Nino, Joseph "Bubba" Butera of Damian's, Elouise Adams Jones of Ouisie's Table, Estella Erdmann of Samba Grille, and Tracy Vaught of Hugo's and Backstreet Cafe.

The following chef/owners who made time to sit and chat about the business: Robert Del Grande of RDG and Bar Annie, Mark Cox of Mark's American Cuisine, Monica Pope of Sparrow Cookshop & Bar, Philippe Schmit of Philippe Restaurant and Lounge, Genevieve Philippe of Bistro Provence, Charles Clark of Ibiza and Brasserie 19, Carlos Ramos of Latin Bites Cafe, Randy Evans of Haven, Anita Jaisinghani of Pondicheri and Indika, David Grossman of Mockingbird Bistro, Claire Smith of Canopy and Shade, Jason Chaney of the Barbed Rose, Vanessa O'Donnell of Ooh La La, Anna Pham and Mai Nguyen of Mai's, Philip Speer of Uchi, and Van Bui and daughter Anny of Huynh.

The managers of the restaurants who went out of their way to make my visits seem effortless: Chris Fannin of Philippe Restaurant and Lounge, David Dworski of Mark's American Cuisine, Kathryne Castellanos of Haven, JoAnn DeNicola of Damian's Cucina Italiana, Haydar Kustu of Hubbell and Hudson Bistro, Gabe Canales of Tony's, Angela Moore of Quattro/Four Seasons Hotel, Scott Sulma of Caio Bello, Naomi Lofton of Ouisie's Table, Tim Taylor of Pizzatola's BBQ, and Jonathan Horowitz of Max's Wine Dive.

Lindsey Brown of the Greater Houston Convention and Visitors Bureau who helped with where chefs eat.

Terry Vine, for his fabulous photography.

John Wilson, for his charming and useful map.

Mick Vann, for hanging in through the food crawls of burgers, Asian food, pizza, and barbecue.

Rachel Dove, my assistant.

And to all of the chefs, cooks, dishwashers, servers, and hosts who work in the Houston food scene.

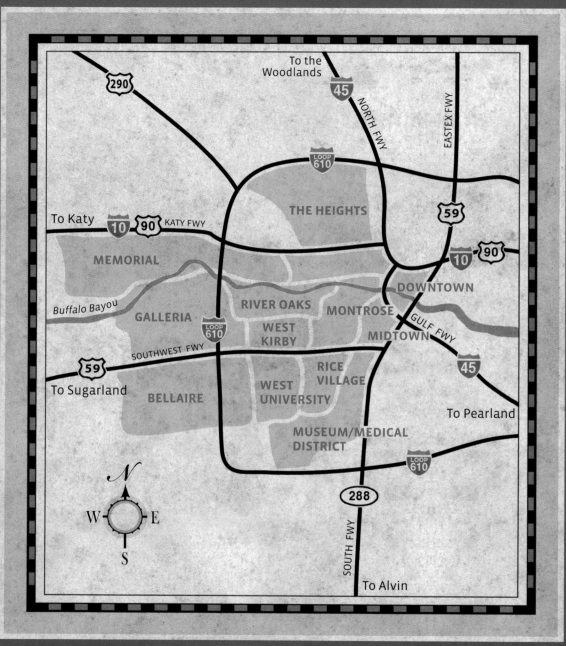

Introduction

Houston is not just the food capital of Texas but also one of the best food cities in America. Key to the quality that Houstonians expect of their restaurants is the food purveyor. So close to the Gulf of Mexico, Houston enjoys some of the freshest seafood available. Small, specialty ranches supply Texas Wagyu beef, heritage pork, and specialty cuts of lamb and goat. Local farmers raise organic vegetables and deliver daily the freshest produce possible. Chefs enjoy wandering through farmers' markets to select something special at the peak of ripeness, flavor, and availability for their menu. Ethnic markets abound and offer specialized produce, herbs, and spices. And what cannot be found locally can be ordered over the Internet and shipped overnight.

Great restaurants start with great ingredients, and the chef is responsible for seeking out consistently superior supplies. With a global market aided by the Internet and overnight shipping worldwide, knowing what is in season and special to every region of the world is an essential skill of a top restaurant's chef when providing the best possible dining experience. As an example, Burgundy truffles are harvested in Italy in a very narrow window of about one month, between the harvest of black truffles and the start of white truffles, usually in September. Featuring them shaved over pasta, with their inimitable aroma released by the warmth of the dish, offers a unique dining experience that cannot be duplicated at home, and it would not be experienced in a restaurant without this knowledge from the master chef.

When it comes to going out for a great meal in Houston, the only problem is deciding which great restaurant to patronize. While the numbers vary depending on whom you ask, there are at least 5,000 traditional restaurants, with some estimates as high as 8,000, in and around the city of Houston.

There are seafood restaurants, steak houses, burger joints, classical French restaurants, modern American, Southwestern, Tex-Mex, Cajun, Creole, soul food, barbecue, regional authentic Mexican, and Central and South American restaurants. We can dine on the cuisines of the Caribbean, Spain, Italy, Belgium, Germany, Poland, Greece, the Mediterranean, Turkey, North and Central Africa, Lebanon, Afghanistan, Persia (Iran), and India.

If you enjoy food from the Pacific Rim, the food of Japan, Korea, China, Singapore, Thailand, Vietnam, Cambodia, the Philippines, Indonesia, and Malaysia are all within driving distance of home. There are twenty-four-hour restaurants, sandwich shops, brew pubs, hot dog stands, delis, kosher and halal restaurants, pizza parlors, family dining places, salad bars, health food and vegetarian restaurants, buffets and cafeterias, bakeries, breakfast joints, and coffeehouses.

HOUSTON'S FOOD STORY

Houston's history can be seen as a map leading to its current status as a national food city based on culinary diversity. Despite Houston's less-than-promising start as the center of Texas's economy and dining, this city has grown to be the largest in Texas and the fourth-largest in the United States, and it is considered the food capital of the state. Established at

NASA

A most famous and often repeated quote is "Houston, we have a problem," from the Ron Howard movie *Apollo 13*, often uttered when an unexpected problem arises in all walks of life. However, this is a misquote of the actual statement made to NASA by Commander Jim Lovell about an oxygen tank that had exploded. The true quote is "Houston, we've had a problem." The misquote seems to have more impact when uttered in the calm, almost blasé voice of a trained professional in a life-or-death situation.

the confluence of the White Oak and Buffalo Bayous in 1836, Houston's real birth came on the heels of the beginning of the twentieth century with the discovery of oil in Beaumont in 1901. Having a ship channel and seventeen railroads, Houston naturally became the hub of modern commerce in Texas and connected the East with the West, bringing people of all ethnic makeup into the city. Investors were drawn to Houston as a place to finance new businesses, and soon Houston became the financial center of Texas as well.

Houston had it all heading into the 1930s—oil and gas, established crops such as sugar cane and rice, a ship channel and major port, railroads to move the commodities, and lots of money to invest in modernization and infrastructure. The 1930s were the beginning of America's modern airline industry, and by 1936 Braniff and Eastern had established hubs in Houston, accelerating the flow of immigrants to the city—which became the largest in Texas in 1939 and never looked back. Houston had become multicultural, and the food and dining scenes soon reflected this. World War II turned common refineries of oil into manufacturing centers of valuable petrochemicals, and this lasted well beyond the end of the conflict. Massive federal spending to finance the war effort brought thousands of workers of all nationalities and economic levels to work in technology-based facilities.

When it came to technology in the 1950s and '60s, nothing could compare to NASA's Manned Spacecraft Center in the Clear Lake area of Houston. The space race was on and all eyes and ears tuned to the skies. When President John F. Kennedy announced the moon landing project, the modest farm-to-market road FM528 became NASA 1, and the most advanced space center in the world displaced the Girl Scout camp that was housed on the property. An influx of technicians of myriad background, along with workers of limited skills but diverse ethnic makeup, rushed to Houston to seek work in this highly funded government venture.

Houston's medical reputation was on the rise as well, with multiple medical centers popping up in the city's landscape. A charitable hospital, funded by George H. Hermann in 1893, eventually became Memorial Hermann Hospital. The University of Texas cancer research center, the Texas Medical Center, and a 1,000-bed naval hospital all started in the 1940s, and by 1954 the Shriner's Hospital, Texas Children's Hospital, Baylor College of Medicine teaching hospital, the Methodist Hospital, St. Luke's Episcopal Hospital, and the Texas Medical Center Library were all serving those in need of first-rate medical care. Today, the Texas Medical Center is the largest medical facility in the world with almost fifty institutions including thirteen hospitals, two medical schools, and schools of nursing, dentistry, pharmacy, and public health. This large healthcare system and the worldwide draw of workers of all skill sets, from surgeons to construction workers, rapidly added to Houston's ethnic and culinary diversity, which heavily influenced the city's food scene.

Today Houston's diversified economy still attracts professionals from around the world in the medical, aerospace, and energy fields. With residents having good jobs and money to spend, restaurants are thriving and can dare to be cutting edge, creative, and ethnically diverse, making dining out in Houston a pleasure-filled experience not available in most cities.

The Keys to Dining Success

So, what makes a successful restaurant, such as one that is included in this book? It starts at the top with the restaurateur, who may or may not also be the chef. This person has a vision that is both broad in scope and specific in detail. He or she understands what diners are looking for in the complete experience, from the decor to the menu, to the level of service and quality and presentation of food.

Great restaurants should offer great service. The serving staff should anticipate your needs. With truly great service you will never notice the personnel performing these tasks. Your meal should move seamlessly from course to course, with just the right amount of time to savor what has just been eaten and to allow it to settle before the next course appears, with no rushing and no waiting. For this to occur, the interaction between the kitchen and the servers must be practiced and coordinated like a fine ballet.

Finally, and most important, great restaurants exist because of the people who support them. If people aren't willing to try a new restaurant, sample the cooking of a new, young chef, or travel a bit to try a new cuisine, then the restaurateurs are less likely to try something new or different. Local news media support is critical as they might feature food topics and regularly promote the area's food scene. Food festivals and music/art venues must be supported by local government too. Thankfully, Houston has all of this and is blessed with one of the most vibrant food scenes in the United States.

HOUSTON'S NEIGHBORHOODS

Houston is the only city in the United States without zoning codes. While this would seem to lead to a discordant arrangement of homes next to oil refineries next to hotels, this is not the case. Strong neighborhood associations and powerful developers have kept this in check over the years.

Houston's social life is driven by neighborhoods, in which people shop, dine out, and reside. Suburbs are quite separate from the neighborhoods in which many Houstonians work and eat. The "Loop" begins to define where to look for suburbs and neighborhoods. I-10 runs from California to Florida, right through Houston, and Interstate Loop 610 forms a ring around the city. Where you are in the city of Houston begins with either "inside the Loop" or "outside the Loop."

River Oaks / Upper Kirby

Houston's tony neighborhood and most impressive address, River Oaks, began as a weekend getaway for the city's wealthy and successful. Huge homes reside on lush, manicured properties along old oak and large tree-lined streets. In addition to mansions, there is great shopping and dining to be found in the River Oaks Shopping Center. Upper Kirby is a neighborhood just south of River Oaks and is sometimes thought of as being joined to it as one large neighborhood, as restaurants and residential areas border each other and are of similar economic status.

Downtown

Houston's downtown has experienced revitalization in recent years, especially with respect to dining, entertainment, and living. For many who work downtown, returning in the evening to have dinner or see a show was just not as appealing as eating in a neighborhood establishment. Today there are excellent restaurants to select from and first-rate entertainment. The Hobby Center for Performing Arts and the Houston Grand Opera, which has been operating since 1955, have become appealing reasons to have dinner and see a show downtown. Houston's light-rail system is efficient and easy to use in getting around the downtown area, making it more convenient for downtown living in one of Houston's expensive lofts and apartments.

Midtown

The area south of downtown has recently been renamed Midtown. A formerly rundown section of downtown has become revitalized with great restaurants and shops. Its border with Montrose is fuzzy, and it is sometimes difficult to know where one begins and the other ends, but what's in a name when the entire area is a satisfying destination for food and shopping? Trendy apartments are springing up and prices are higher than in Montrose, but there are accessible supermarkets and other conveniences missing in Montrose. Midtown houses a large and growing Vietnamese population, with ethnic shops and restaurants to enjoy.

Washington Avenue

This corridor is one of the hottest regions for new restaurants and bars. In addition condos and town houses are popping up nearby, supplying first homes to young, successful families. It has been a rundown neighborhood for years and is now relishing a rebirth. The road was a former stagecoach and pioneer wagon trail used to enter Houston's downtown and is now a destination for fine dining and barhopping. The eclectic mix still includes some seedy portions, but that is sure to change as young chefs, restaurateurs, and entrepreneurs find reasonable rents and potential in the buildings that exist along the Avenue. Connecting streets usher you into Montrose and River Oaks in minutes, and downtown is also just a short drive away.

The Heights

The Heights, just northwest of downtown and inside the Loop, was Houston's first planned community. It was meant for people to escape the crowded conditions of the city itself, and in some ways was considered a Utopian-style community. To this day alcohol is banned and the neighborhood is "dry." Restaurants and bars get around this restriction—as do many US counties that are dry—by establishing "clubs" with "members" in order to sell

WHERE CHEFS EAT

We know where they work, and it's interesting to know where they go when they are hungry. It may surprise you that chefs do not seek out finely crafted foods, made by skilled and highly trained culinary professionals. That is what they do all day long! Instead, they seek big flavor, reasonable price, fast service, often using ingredients not usually found in their pantry and cooking techniques not often utilized by them during work. Take Asian food as an example. To cook a stir-fry properly one needs a wok burner flame under their wok. This specialized burner has no substitute, as its heat output is five times that of a commercial 30,000 BTU burner (which has the output of three times that of a home range). If it's Thai you want, you will probably not have galangal root, fresh lemongrass, and makroot leaf handy. It's so much better to hang up your apron, jump into your car, and drive to any one of a multitude of excellent Thai restaurants that specialize in this cuisine.

Chefs like their restaurants to be open early so they can grab something on the way into their kitchen or to stay open late after they have finished their dinner shift and their kitchen is closed, or to be fast and nourishing to grab a quick bite between lunch and dinner service. The good news is that they like the places you like to eat at as well—burger joints, Asian restaurants of all ethnicities, pizzerias, and barbecue restaurants are particular favorites of theirs. Look throughout the text for Where Chefs Eat sidebars that cover restaurants in each of these categories.

Keep in mind that each of these categories has variations by which people tend to be polarized. For example, when discussing great pizza, crust style can be the deal breaker. Deep-dish or thin crust is always an issue. Is it cooked in an "authentic" wood-burning, brick-lined oven or a typical stainless steel pizza oven? Is the mozzarella fresh or grated from loaves? Is the sauce sweet, complex, or just crushed tomatoes? The list can go on and on, but the true foodie will appreciate a great deep-dish pie because it is great, and still prefer the Neapolitan thin-crust style. The same is true for barbecue, burgers, and Thai food.

Chefs are like everyone else. They have their preferences and idiosyncrasies, but can appreciate excellence based on a multitude of styles.

alcoholic beverages. The Heights gets its name from being 23 feet above the elevation of downtown Houston, which is prone to serious flooding being in the Gulf coastal plain (and the 100-year flood plain). Today it is an eclectic mix of large homes, small bungalows, quirky shops, and a rising restaurant destination.

Montrose

If you are looking for character, you can't beat Montrose. Originally a planned community in the early 1900s, the streets and boulevards were constructed especially wide, with fine sidewalks and a streetcar system running through the district. Many mansions were built here, and few remain today. By the 1970s Montrose became known for its "alternative" lifestyles and to this day is considered the most eclectic and liberal-thinking section of Houston. The Houston Pride Festival and Parade are hosted by Montrose every June, celebrating the GLBT community, which has begun to decline in Montrose and increase its presence in the Heights. Montrose has great restaurants, eclectic shopping, and reasonably priced housing. It borders Downtown, Midtown, River Oaks, and Rice Village, all within minutes of this district. To capture the feeling of early Montrose, drive by the Colombe d'Or Hotel at 3410 Montrose Boulevard, the former home of the Walter Fondren family, founders of Humble Oil. Better yet, dine at its fine restaurant CINQ and marvel at the interior.

Galleria

The mall at Galleria is one of America's largest and is known for fine shopping and high-end stores. It is one of Houston's most popular tourist destinations. Restaurants abound but there are few bars and clubs. The Galleria mall opened in 1970 and was inspired by the Galleria Vittorio Emanuel II shopping center in Milan, Italy. In addition to shopping there are office towers attached to the mall and upscale hotels, such as the Derek and ICON, are located nearby as are the lion's share of visitors' hotels serving the Greater Houston area. The Loop cuts through the Galleria with the larger portion outside the Loop. The neighborhood is often referred to as Uptown and is the financial center of Houston, with tall office buildings deceiving travelers that they have arrived in Downtown Houston, still miles away.

Rice Village/West University

Surrounding Rice University is Rice Village, a neighborhood of students and young couples, of retail shopping, reasonably priced restaurants, and bars. This is the social hub for young Houstonians. West "U," as it is called, adjoins Rice Village but has a different demographic due to its history. It turned from a middle-class neighborhood to one in which "yuppies" would take over and rebuild its modest mid-20th-century bungalows into a rather wealthy neighborhood. Those who could not afford the rapidly increasing taxes moved west to what is now Bellaire, a more affordable community.

Museum District / Medical Center

The area south of Montrose is home to Houston's most popular museums and beautiful park. Montrose Boulevard terminates at a traffic circle, and the Houston Museum of Natural Science is directly ahead as is Hermann Park, which contains the Houston Zoo. Just north of the circle and Mecom Fountain is the Jung Center for Education, the Contemporary Arts Museum Houston, and the Museum of Fine Arts. This is a popular neighborhood for a stroll with the kids or a leisurely walk on a cool day. To the east of the Museum District is the Texas Medical Center, the largest in the world with fourteen patient care institutions including Children's Memorial Hermann Hospital, Texas Children's Hospital, and the M.D. Anderson Cancer Center. Fifteen academic and research institutions are housed in the Texas Medical Center, such as the Baylor College of Medicine, the Texas Heart Institute, and the Texas Medical Library. There are numerous hotel and dining options to serve visitors and patients' families.

Memorial

Memorial is one of the wealthiest neighborhoods of Houston. It is divided into five villages that operate separately from the city of Houston, having their own police and fire departments. Unlike River Oaks, Memorial has been in development only since the 1960s and is mainly outside the Loop. Its development began as upper-middle-class homes along the Buffalo Bayou. The "Energy Corridor" is located here and Memorial is the preferred neighborhood. In the 1970s major companies looked to the suburbs to relocate and Shell Oil and Conoco were the first to arrive. Soon Amoco and Exxon joined in opening campuses here. The Energy Corridor District was established in 2001.

The Suburbs

Houston is as spread out as a city can be, and many have heard of the commuting nightmares on the vast expanse of highways and tollways. Constant construction both relieves and exacerbates the problem. With many smaller cities the suburbs are usually no more than five to ten miles from the heart of the city; in Houston the two most populous suburbs are Katy and the Woodlands, both requiring more than twenty miles of commuting. The commute to and from Katy has been one success of highway construction. Not only are there as many as six lanes along I-10 between downtown and the Katy exits, but there is also a toll lane with automatic scanning toll booths overhead and an HOV lane to relieve the pressure of the commuting onslaught at rush hours.

Katy's history begins as an agricultural community, with rice being the major crop. The Missouri, Kansas and Texas Railway gave the boost to establish Katy as a city with the US Postal Service. Katy is named for the railroad that gave it such a start. By the 1940s Katy became the site of one of the largest gas fields in America, giving a tremendous boost to its economy. Today Katy has the charm of a small town with the sophistication of a suburban location to a large city.

In 1974 the Woodlands became a master-planned community, specifically as a suburban development to Houston. Corporations soon were attracted to the region, where a conference center, hotels, golf courses, retail malls, and schools were planned. One way to attract residents is through an excellent school system, and the Woodlands has succeeded in this. From preschools to the Academy for Lifelong Learning for seniors, there are educational opportunities for everyone. The public schools are exemplary, as are the private schools. Lone Star College–University Center and Montgomery offer undergraduate and graduate education. With over 100 parks and almost 200 miles of trails, outdoor activities abound. The Woodlands has successfully prevented annexation by the city of Houston by forming a Township.

In Harris County, Pasadena is considered Houston's most populous suburb (unless, of course, you consider it to be its own city). Nevertheless, it is the heart of Houston's petrochemical industry located by the ship channel. Cypress, unincorporated and northwest of downtown, exists as almost entirely single-family homes, with the second largest school district in metro-Houston. It continues to be one of the fastest-growing suburban regions in the area. Jersey City and Tomball, also northwest, are a fairly short commute to downtown. To the southwest Sugarland is a fast-growing and wealthy city, housing high-tech firms and energy companies, with many master-planned communities. Directly south and the nearest suburb to the medical center and downtown is Pearland, home to professionals in the aerospace, energy, and medical professions.

BACKSTREET CAFE

MONTROSE/NEARTOWN
1103 SOUTH SHEPHERD DRIVE
(713) 521-2239
WWW.BACKSTREETCAFE.NET
CHEF: HUGO ORTEGA
OWNER: TRACY VAUGHT

For any restaurant to be open for almost thirty years, it must be doing something right. Actually, Hector Ortega, the general manager, will tell you it's two things. Stay poised to reinvent yourself as trends occur and, most important, listen to your guests. According to Ortega, "Everything comes from the guests." With this philosophy it is no surprise that service is outstanding here. It is attentive without being obtrusive. Guests are urged to fill out comment cards and to give input at any time.

Backstreet fills with regulars, neighborhood folks, and stylish, young, successful Houstonians. They come for the food, of course, and Chef Hugo Ortega (no relation) provides seasonal menus that adapt to available produce. In addition to four menus reflecting the seasons, there are sub-menus that feature something that is immediately in season, such as the separate artichoke menu resting on all tables. There are twenty dishes featuring artichokes, from sublime baby artichoke and kale chowder with root vegetables to shrimp-stuffed artichoke bottoms or the best artichoke dip you've ever had. Chef Ortega supports the Urban Harvest Market, from where he obtains his specialty produce, and every Sunday he offers a three-course menu based on what he found in the market the previous day. He also donates five dollars back to the Urban Market for each dinner sold. The menus at Backstreet Cafe can be described as New American, and their Saturday brunch menu is just that. Offerings include grilled bacon-wrapped quail, roasted pear and blue cheese salad, pecan-crusted chicken, crawfish grits cakes with poached eggs, and a crispy lobster sandwich on homemade brioche, just to name a few. Be sure to ask for the current flavor of lemonade; the watermelon lemonade is delightful.

Bosc pears are perfect for cooking as they hold their shape quite well. They are in season from September to April. Their smooth texture and honey sweet flesh pair well with wine and cheese, as cleverly done in this tasty recipe. The house dressing is versatile and should be part of your salad repertoire.

Stuffed Poached Pear Salad
with Blue Cheese, Dried Fruits & Nuts

SERVES 4

For the house dressing (makes 1 cup):

¾ cup olive oil, divided
7 anchovies, coarsely chopped
1 small carrot, peeled and diced
¼ large red pepper, seeded and coarsely chopped
½ cup sliced mushrooms
½ large shallot, diced
1 garlic clove, minced

For the salad:

1 cup Port wine
¾ cup demi-glace
½ cup maple syrup
¼ cup house dressing (see above)
4 ripe Bosc pears, peeled
¼ cup pecans
¼ cup walnuts
¼ cup dried cranberries
2 tablespoons crumbled blue cheese
16 red oak lettuce leaves
2 bunches watercress, rinsed and picked over
Blue cheese for garnish
Dried cranberries for garnish
1 tablespoon freshly ground black pepper
2 oil-packed sun-dried tomatoes, coarsely chopped
1 tablespoon chopped kalamata olives
3 tablespoons cider vinegar
3 tablespoons champagne wine vinegar
¼ cup chiffonade fresh basil
1 green onion, chopped

To prepare the dressing, add ¼ cup olive oil to a large sauté pan and place over medium-high heat. Add the anchovies, carrot, red pepper, mushrooms, shallot, and garlic and sauté for 3 minutes, lowering the heat if necessary. Remove from heat and allow the mixture to cool completely.

For the salad, add the wine, demi-glace, maple syrup, and house dressing to a large nonreactive saucepan. Stir the mixture until uniform. Bring the liquid to a boil over medium-high heat.

Add the pears to the liquid, lower the heat to a simmer, and cover. Poach the pears until they are soft, about 30 to 35 minutes. Remove the pears to a sheet pan or tray and allow them to cool. Remove and dispose of the cores and set the pears aside.

Strain the poaching liquid and transfer about half to a small saucepan, discarding the rest. Simmer the liquid under low heat until it reaches a syrup consistency, about 1 hour. Set aside.

Add the pecans, walnuts, dried cranberries, and 2 tablespoons of crumbled blue cheese to a small food processor. Pulse to combine.

Fill each pear with 2 tablespoons of the nut mixture. Arrange 4 red oak lettuce leaves on each plate. Place a stuffed pear in the center and drizzle about 2 tablespoons of reduced liquid over each pear. Scatter each plate with watercress and garnish with crumbled blue cheese and dried cranberries.

Transfer the mixture to a food processor and add the black pepper, sun-dried tomatoes, kalamata olives, both vinegars, the basil, and green onions. Gently pulse the mixture until the ingredients are finely chopped but not puréed.

Transfer the ingredients to a bowl and slowly whisk in the remaining ½ cup olive oil to emulsify the dressing.

This recipe is hearty enough for a dinner meal or a Sunday brunch. Adding leftover roast chicken or turkey works well in this dish.

SMOKED CHICKEN & POTATO HASH
WITH POACHED EGGS

SERVES 4

For the hash:

2 tablespoons olive oil

1 small shallot, peeled and thinly sliced

2 garlic cloves, peeled and thinly sliced

4 small tomatillos, husks removed, washed, thinly sliced

1½ cups mashed potatoes (leftovers work well)

1 whole smoked/roasted chicken, meat pulled from
     the carcass, shredded

1 green onion, sliced

2 roasted red peppers, peeled, seeded, finely diced

¼ bunch cilantro, finely chopped

8 poached eggs

8 warm flour tortillas

8 slices ripe avocado

For the salsa (makes 1 cup):

2 medium tomatillos, husks removed,
     washed, quartered

¼ bunch cilantro, coarsely chopped

2 tablespoons minced white onion

1 small Serrano pepper, stem removed,
     seeded, deveined, coarsely chopped

½ medium avocado, cut into ½-inch pieces

1 teaspoon lime juice

¾ teaspoon salt

Add the olive oil to a large sauté pan over medium heat. Add the shallot and garlic and sauté lightly, being careful not to burn the garlic.

Add the tomatillos and mashed potatoes, allowing the mixture to brown while stirring, about 1 minute.

Add the shredded chicken, green onion, and roasted red peppers. Sauté for 2 minutes. Stir in the cilantro.

For the salsa add the tomatillos, cilantro, onion, and Serrano pepper to a food processor and pulse to combine (do not purée).

Add the avocado, lime juice, and salt and pulse briefly, leaving the salsa with some texture.

Divide the hash among 4 plates. Accompany each plate with 2 poached eggs and 2 warm flour tortillas, rolled. Garnish each plate with 2 slices of avocado. Top each plate's poached eggs with 2 tablespoons of salsa.

Barbed Rose

ALVIN
113 EAST SEALY STREET
(281) 585-2272
WWW.BARBEDROSE.COM
CHEF/OWNER: JASON CHANEY

Every Texas steak house should be like the Barbed Rose. In addition to being warm and inviting, the decor is tastefully subdued Texan, including the music. The staff is sincerely Texas friendly. Every item served is house-made, including the mustards, ketchup, relishes, breads, sandwich buns, bacon, and all charcuterie. The hot dogs are made from Texas Wagyu beef trimmings and are served on freshly baked pretzel bread buns topped with nigella seeds. The Barbed Rose is in farm country, about 30 minutes from downtown Houston, in the historic district of Alvin, Texas. Local growers show up at the kitchen back door with the harvest of the day, and are willing to grow whatever Chef/Owner Jason Chaney desires. Chef Chaney also sources the Barbed Rose's protein from regional purveyors including Texas Wagyu beef and succulent lamb from Yocum.

The menu is Texas/Gulf Coast inspired, so be sure to start your meal with country-fried Gulf oysters, resting on house-made bacon, topped with pickled jalapeños that have been locally harvested. Experience Barbed Rose's charcuterie skills with a sampler plate of bacon, pepperoni, summer sausage, and spicy link sausage. Feel free to create your own entree by selecting from a list of sauces (blueberry demi-glace, mint chimichurri, pequillo pepper beurre blanc, or nine others equally as delicious-sounding) to top your selection of beef (Angus, Wagyu, Akaushi), Berkshire pork, Strauss veal, Texas antelope, bison, axis venison, wild boar, quail, ostrich, diver scallops, rock shrimp, or six others. Or allow the chef to make your decision by ordering the nut- and panko-crusted Scottish salmon, barbecued shrimp and grits, or a half free-range chicken with bacon tomato jam. The owners of the Barbed Rose are planning a complete dining district in Alvin with an artisanal bakery and butcher shop to complement the restaurant.

Texas Cobb Salad

SERVES 4

For the vinaigrette (makes 3 cups):

1 cup whole grain mustard
3 tablespoons minced shallots
²/₃ cup agave nectar
¹/₃ cup rice wine vinegar
1 cup extra-virgin olive oil
Salt and pepper

For the salad:

3–4 hearts romaine, leaves separated, washed,
 and torn into 1-inch pieces
¾ cup agave mustard vinaigrette (see above)
2 hard-boiled eggs, peeled and chopped
1 avocado, peeled and diced
4 ounces crisp cooked bacon, crumbled
4 ounces crumbled Texas (or other) goat cheese
1 medium tomato, seeded and diced
4 ounces cooked, blackened chicken breast, diced
1 ear fresh corn, roasted, kernels removed
¼ cup rinsed and chopped fresh cilantro
Salt and pepper

To make the vinaigrette, place the mustard, shallots, agave nectar, and rice wine vinegar in a large bowl. Slowly whisk in the oil to emulsify.

Adjust seasoning with salt and pepper. Can be held, refrigerated, for 1 week.

Toss the lettuce with the vinaigrette dressing until thoroughly coated.

Add chopped eggs, diced avocado, bacon, goat cheese, tomato, chicken, corn, and cilantro. Toss gently. Add salt and pepper to taste.

Divide the salad among 4 chilled plates and serve immediately.

SMOKED PEPPER STEAK

SERVES 4

Unlike the typical pepper steak, this dish has Asian influence. Shishito peppers are thin-skinned green chiles about 3 to 4 inches long and can be consumed in their entirety, seeds and all. They tend to be fairly mild, but occasionally you will bite into a fiery one. Banana peppers would make a good substitute.

3 pounds rib eye roast, excess fat removed
1 cup sweet soy sauce
¼ cup hoisin sauce
1 tablespoon grated fresh ginger
2 tablespoons chopped scallions
2 tablespoons minced cilantro
2 tablespoons Asian fish sauce
10 ounces shishito peppers
Coarse salt

Cold smoke the rib eye roast (under 100°F) for 2 hours and chill. (In cold smoking the smoke is generated in a chamber separate from the food, so there is no heat transfer to what is being smoked, just smoke flavor.)

Mix the sweet soy sauce, hoisin sauce, ginger, scallions, cilantro, and fish sauce together.

Cut the roast into 4 steaks and grill over coals to desired doneness.

Add the peppers to a very hot, dry skillet and stir until just charred all over. Sprinkle with coarse salt.

Serve the steaks with portions of charred peppers and sauce drizzled over the steaks.

BENJY'S UPPER WASHINGTON

WASHINGTON AVENUE
5922 WASHINGTON AVENUE
(713) 868-1131
WWW.BENJYS.COM
CHEF: MIKE POTOWSKI
OWNER: BENJY LEVIT

Benjy's is a perfect reflection of the renovated and rejuvenated neighborhood of Washington Avenue. Its living room casual design draws the local residents in droves. And why not? The emphasis is on local produce and regional goods. The menu is eclectic without being silly. Chef Mike Potowski draws on his background of Japanese-Lithuanian with a Polish family name to come up with just the right combination of flavors and textures to tantalize the palate without overpowering the featured ingredients. He respects his vegetables with a delicate touch and thoughtful combination. Fried Brussels sprouts with banyuls vinegar and Parmesan may be the best vegetable dish ever.

The tone of Chef Potowski's menu is earthy as he searches out the freshest possible locally grown ingredients. The frenetic pace in the kitchen does not filter into the dining room; the food comes to table effortlessly and belies the complexity of the component parts of each dish.

One great way to enjoy dining at benjy's is to hang out on the patio deck upstairs and have one of their fabulous pizzas. Try a nontraditional pizza with calamari and drizzled with coconut mango aioli. The bar carries the cocktail offerings to a new level by making infusions of standard labels with herbs, spices, and savory components to produce unique flavor profiles. Also, additional barrel-aging is given to fine whiskeys to make them ultra-smooth. The effort must be working because benjy's has received such awards as Best Bar from *Playboy* magazine and Best Happy Hour and Best Martini from CitySearch.com.

Red Snapper Sashimi with Pickled Grapes

SERVES 4

The fish used in sashimi must be of the highest quality and freshness. Feel free to substitute any sashimi-grade fish you can obtain. The pickled grapes go well with rich meats, such as roast pork.

½ cup rice vinegar

½ cup sugar

10 whole cloves

1 teaspoon ground cardamom

2 bay leaves

2 star anise

½ teaspoon sea salt

½ cup red seedless grapes

1 (8-ounce) red snapper fillet, sashimi grade

3 tablespoons white soy sauce

3 tablespoons water

1 tablespoon minced chives

2 tablespoons grape seed oil

1 tablespoon minced and seeded jalapeño

Sea salt

1 teaspoon peeled, fine julienne ginger

¼ cup peppery greens, such as arugula or tatsoi

2 tablespoons fresh lemon juice

2 tablespoons fruity olive oil

Add the rice vinegar, sugar, cloves, cardamom, bay leaves, star anise, and sea salt to a small saucepan and bring to a boil. Simmer 2 minutes.

Strain the liquid and pour over the grapes. Allow to cool and refrigerate 8 hours.

Slice the snapper very thin and place in a nonreactive bowl. Add the white soy sauce, water, chives, grape seed oil, and jalapeño. Season lightly with sea salt and toss gently to combine. Refrigerate 1 hour.

Add 2-ounce portions of snapper to small plates. Arrange the ginger, greens, and pickled grapes on top. Mix the lemon juice and olive oil together and drizzle over each plate. Top each dish with a little more sea salt and serve immediately.

BISTRO ALEX

CITY CENTRE
800 SORELLA COURT
(713) 827-3545
WWW.BISTROALEX.COM
CHEF: ROLANDO SOZA
OWNER: HOTEL SORELLA

No one does "new" like Houston does new. After the fading out of a large shopping center on the west side of the city in the 1980s due to the opening of the fabulous Galleria closer to town, developers created City Centre, a sparkling new development of condos, town homes, a hotel, restaurants, and shops. This center serves the Energy Corridor, home to ExxonMobil and Shell Oil. One of Houston's most beautiful neighborhoods lies just to the south. City Centre is pedestrian friendly and a convenient way to shop and eat.

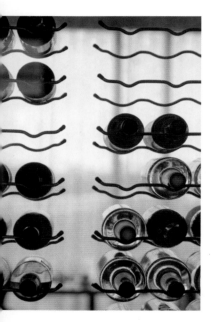

At its heart is the Hotel Sorella, a modern and friendly place to stay, with large, spotless, welcoming rooms and a staff that aims to please. One of the best things about the hotel is its restaurant, Bistro Alex, named for Alex Brennan Martin of the famous Brennan family of restaurants. The restaurant is modern in decor with chrome and grays dominating the interior. A striking wall of wines greets each guest in a corridor leading to the dining room. They offer an interesting version of a chef's table, a long bar with comfortable stools, allowing guests to view the action in the kitchen while they dine.

While there are some of Brennan's favorites on the menu, such as turtle soup, Chef Soza believes in bold flavors and straightforward preparations that augment New Orleans cuisine, which reflects his personality quite nicely. The fried green tomatoes topped with succulent lump crab are a perfect way to start the meal.

If you like to nibble, the charcuterie plate is for you. All meats, hams, sausages, and pâtés are house-made, and the Tasso ham is both delicate and spicy. Accompanying cheeses are from Texas's best cheese makers, the Veldhuizen family. The crab cake is unique in that there is absolutely no filler; it is 100 percent crab with seasonings and spices, formed into a tower. Fish is from the Gulf and filleted on-site. The bar jack is delicate and meaty, served on a bed of Louisiana's famous *maque choux,* a corn sauté with tomatoes and spices, and in this rendition, crabmeat is added as a lagniappe (bonus treat).

Do not miss the dessert offerings. In addition to a rich chocolate mousse dome, the tea cake with berries macerated in *limoncello* is wonderful. An aromatic apple cobbler, right from the oven, topped with a crunchy crumble and a scoop of homemade vanilla ice cream, effuses the essence of autumn.

Tea Cake with Marinated Strawberries

SERVES 8–12

This cake is quite rich, and small servings are quite filling. Marzipan may be substituted for almond paste and can be found in bulk in Middle Eastern markets. Other fruit such as raspberries or blueberries can replace the strawberries. Limoncello is the second most popular liqueur in Italy and is produced in the south from the zest of Sorrento lemons. A glass of limoncello would make a perfect accompaniment to this dessert.

For the cake:

1 pound unsalted butter
3 cups sugar
11 ounces almond paste
2 tablespoons vanilla
10 eggs
2 cups flour
1 teaspoon baking powder
1 teaspoon salt

For the marinated strawberries:

3 pints strawberries
1 cup sugar
¼ cup limoncello liqueur

To serve:

Whipped cream
Candied lemon peel

Beat the butter with the sugar until light and fluffy. Add the almond paste and continue to beat until incorporated.

Whisk in the vanilla and the eggs, adding one at a time, waiting until each is incorporated.

Sift the flour with the baking powder and salt and stir it into the butter mixture, forming a smooth batter.

Bake in a well-greased tube pan or Bundt pan at 300°F for 45 minutes or until set in the center. Allow to cool in the pan on a wire rack.

For the marinated strawberries, remove the green tops and quarter each. Cut each quarter in half.

Add the sugar and limoncello and stir to incorporate. Allow to stand at room temperature 2 hours, stirring occasionally. Refrigerate until thoroughly chilled.

To serve, place a slice of tea cake on a plate. Surround with marinated strawberries and top with whipped cream. Add candied lemon peel as garnish.

Foie Gras Torchon

SERVES 12

To make a torchon, food is wrapped tightly in a kitchen towel or cheesecloth to hold delicate ingredients together so as to not lose shape or crumble during preparation. Foie gras is an ideal candidate for this technique, compressing the tender liver and allowing it to be sliced perfectly for presentation.

About 1½ pounds grade A foie gras
2 quarts whole milk
2 teaspoons salt
½ teaspoon sugar
¼ teaspoon white pepper
6 cups apple juice or pineapple juice

Place the foie gras in a container with the milk. Cover and refrigerate 24 hours.

Remove the foie gras from the milk and split the lobes apart. Scrape any film that has formed and carefully remove any veins, leaving the lobes intact.

Season with salt, sugar, and white pepper. Wrap the lobes tightly in plastic film. Refrigerate 24 hours.

Unwrap the foie gras and rewrap in cheesecloth. Heat the apple juice to a simmer and drop the foie gras into the simmering liquid for 2 minutes. Remove to an ice bath and allow to cool.

Wrap the poached foie gras in a clean kitchen towel and tie the ends. Hang it in the refrigerator for 24 hours.

Slice as needed, serving with toasts, jams, and/ or preserved fruits. Wrap the remaining foie gras in plastic film and store in the refrigerator up to 1 week.

Bistro Provence

Memorial
13616 Memorial Drive
(713) 827-8008
www.bistroprovence.us
Chef/Owners: Jean and Genevieve Philippe

Tucked into a small boutique strip center in Memorial is a small but notable taste of southern France. This is authentic Provençal cooking, and they have been dishing it up for over thirteen years at this location to some of Houston's most critical diners of French cuisine, transplanted French citizens, drawn to work in the Energy Corridor of Texas. This is a neighborhood bistro, and it is not uncommon to hear French spoken at many of the tables around you. That it has been open for more than thirteen years speaks highly of the quality and authenticity of the cuisine, as well as the reasonable prices not often seen on French restaurant menus.

Chef/Owner Jean Philippe and his wife, Genevieve, took over the restaurant from his parents about six years ago and it hasn't skipped a beat. In addition to the food, Bistro Provence offers a fascinating wine list of strictly French labels. Noteworthy are the selections from Bandol, which most Houstonians have never had the pleasure of tasting. As the wines are from coastal southern France, they pair perfectly with Provençal cooking. A crisp white wine goes well with the *moules Provençales*, fresh mussels sautéed with shallots, tomatoes, and the sparkle of green peppercorns. The house-baked bread (*fougasse*) is perfect for mopping up the sauce after the mussels have been eaten. The *verrine niçoise* offers layers of tapenade (an olive and anchovy relish), diced tomatoes in olive oil, and a topping of seared tuna. Unlike other regional French cuisines, Provençal cooking relies on fruity olive oil, citrus, and herbs such as lavender, thyme, and basil for its basis, as well as tomatoes and olives. Fresh fish and game provide the protein. As an example the *filet de cabillaud* is a perfectly cooked fillet of fresh cod, marinated in citrus juice resting atop a potato salad dressed with olive oil and seasoned with coriander seed.

Heartier fare includes lamb shanks with rosemary and honey, beef stew with olives, tomatoes, and sweet peppers and a not-to-be-missed fork-tender Moulard duck leg (*cuisse de canard confit*), poached and preserved in its own fat. As a change of pace try their wood-fired oven pizzas. For dessert the lavender-infused crème brulee shouldn't be missed. They offer special Christmas Eve and New Year's Eve menus, which are three courses prix fixe.

PROVENÇAL MUSSELS

MOULES PROVENÇALES

SERVES 2

If fresh mussels are not available, consider frozen ones, which are a surprisingly good alternative. Green lip mussels from New Zealand can be found in many supermarkets' frozen fish section.

¼ cup olive oil
30 Prince Edward mussels (or other variety as available)
1 cup white wine
2 teaspoons green peppercorns
1 large tomato, seeded and chopped
1 shallot, sliced
2 garlic cloves, peeled and minced
½ cup chopped flat-leaf parsley
Salt and pepper

Heat a large, deep pot until very hot. Add the olive oil and then the mussels. Sauté until the mussels begin to open.

Add white wine, peppercorns, tomatoes, shallots, and garlic. Cook until mussels are fully opened.

Season with salt and pepper. Garnish with chopped parsley and serve in a bowl with crusty bread on the side, if desired. Discard any unopened mussels.

CITRUS-MARINATED FRESH COD FILLET WITH CORIANDER POTATO SALAD

SERVES 4

This recipe works well with many firm-fleshed fish, including swordfish. Tangerine segments make a tasty addition to the dish.

Juice of 1 orange
Juice of 1 lemon
¼ cup extra-virgin olive oil
4 (7-ounce) cod fillets

For the potatoes:

10 Red Bliss potatoes, quartered, skins left on
½ teaspoon coriander seed, crushed with the back of a knife
2 tablespoons extra-virgin olive oil
Salt and pepper

For the vinaigrette:

½ cup orange juice
1 tablespoon Dijon mustard
1 teaspoon honey
1½ cups fruity extra-virgin olive oil
Pure olive oil for sautéing

To serve:

1 orange, peeled with pith removed and divided into segments
1 red grapefruit, peeled with pith removed and divided into segments
1 teaspoon coriander seeds, crushed with the back of a knife
3 fresh basil leaves, minced

In a large nonreactive bowl, whisk the orange and lemon juices together with the olive oil. Add the cod fillets, turning to thoroughly coat. Marinate for 4 to 5 hours, refrigerated, turning occasionally.

Bring a large pot of salted water to a boil. Add the quartered potatoes and cook until tender, about 10 minutes. Rinse under cold water. Allow to cool and refrigerate until chilled (can be done 1 day ahead).

Toss the potatoes with 1/2 teaspoon crushed coriander and the extra-virgin olive oil. Return to refrigerator until ready to serve. Adjust seasoning with salt and pepper before service.

For the vinaigrette, whisk the orange juice, mustard, and honey together. Slowly whisk in 1½ cups fruity olive oil to form an emulsion.

Add a few tablespoons of pure olive oil to a large skillet. Pat the marinated cod fillets dry and sauté over high heat about 2 minutes per side or until just flaking.

To serve, add portions of potato salad to each plate. Top with a cod fillet. Arrange citrus segments on each plate and drizzle with vinaigrette. Sprinkle coriander and basil over. Serve immediately.

SPECIAUX DU MIDI

x GAZPACHO 7,

x SALADE DE FRUITS DE MER
MER MIXED GREENS, PETITE
SKEWER OF SHRIMP, SCALLOP
12 CITRUS VINAIGRETTE

BRANCH WATER TAVERN

WASHINGTON AVENUE
510 SHEPHERD DRIVE
(713) 863-7777
WWW.BRANCHWATERTAVERN.COM
CHEF/OWNER: DAVID GROSSMAN

Just off Washington Avenue, a gem of a restaurant has taken over a rather seedy pool hall and turned it into a clubby, inviting dining venue. With warm, dark wood reclaimed from old timber from East Texas, and thick, brick walls, the Branch Water Tavern welcomes you to sit and enjoy the cooking of Chef/Owner David Grossman. Branch Water seemed the perfect name, as the bar specializes in whiskeys, offering a comprehensive list from which to choose. The lighting is perfect—not too dark so as to need a flashlight to read the exciting menu and not too bright.

As soon as you are seated, staff will serve you a treat of fresh, warm biscuits accompanied by homemade pepper jelly. Before opening the Tavern, Chef Grossman worked at Gravitas in Houston, refining his skills. Chef Grossman relies on simple presentations and just the right amount and number of ingredients. The sautéed flounder fillet, on a bed of simply poached vegetables, is accompanied by a generous smear of puréed carrot. In order to protect the flavor and color of fresh carrots, they are cooked *sous vide*, under vacuum and at very low temperature. The treatment makes for a vibrant, intensely flavored sauce that is surprisingly perfect with the flounder. Chicken-fried oysters, topped with celery root slaw and a dash of Frank's Red Hot pepper sauce, is simplicity defined, yet the contrast of slippery, smooth oysters with crunchy slaw is flawless in execution.

STICKY TOFFEE PUDDING
WITH TOFFEE SAUCE

MAKES 8 SERVINGS

Dates are quite nutritious, and you can convince yourself and others that this luxurious dessert is actually good for you. Dates are low in fat but provide a rich mouth feel, and are high in fiber, about 8 percent by weight. The toffee sauce is easy to prepare and stores well, so feel free to double the recipe and have some on hand to drizzle over waffles, pancakes, or a scoop of your favorite ice cream.

For the pudding:

1 cup dates, blanched and peeled
1¼ cups water
1 teaspoon vanilla extract
1 teaspoon baking soda
1 egg, beaten
5 tablespoons softened butter,
    plus additional for molds
¾ cup granulated sugar
2 cups all-purpose flour
1 teaspoon baking powder
¼ teaspoon salt

For the toffee sauce:

½ cup unsalted butter
¾ cup cream
1 1/3 cups dark brown sugar, firmly packed
2 tablespoons dark rum, or to taste

To serve:

1 pint pistachio ice cream

Combine the dates with the water, vanilla, and baking soda. Heat the mixture to a simmer and cook 5 minutes. Remove from heat. Allow to cool and chill thoroughly.

Process the date mixture with the beaten egg to form a smooth paste.

Cream butter and sugar in an electric mixer with paddle attachment until light and fluffy.

Mix the flour, baking powder, and salt together. Add the dry ingredients to the date mixture in portions, mixing until uniform.

Butter and flour 8 (4-ounce) fluted molds and fill each with the date mixture. Bake at 300°F for 20 minutes. Allow to cool and then unmold.

Prepare the toffee sauce by combining all ingredients in a nonreactive saucepan. Heat to a simmer and cook 2 to 3 minutes.

Serve with warm toffee sauce and pistachio ice cream.

BRASSERIE 19

River Oaks
1962 West Gray Street
(713) 524-1919
www.brasserie19.com
Chef: Amanda McGraw
Owner: Charles Clark

Although tucked into a strip center in the busiest section of West Gray, Brasserie 19 feels remarkably like a neighborhood restaurant, complete with excellent service and friendly staff. The "19" in the name references the River Oaks zip code ending. The restaurant's bright white cane chairs and linen with marble-top tables add to the relaxed atmosphere.

The food is impeccably fresh and biased toward fish and seafood, with classic French offerings of cassoulet, beef bourguignon, veal blanquette, and foie gras as well. Steak tartare is hand-cut and not chopped, the perfect way to maintain the flavor of quality beef. The meat is folded into a caper remoulade and topped with a fresh quail egg. A side of frisée salad and Dijon vinaigrette is the proper foil to rich beef. For the adventurous, try the pan-seared frogs' legs with anchovy butter appetizer or cured sweetbreads with pickled plums and Maker's Mark infused pound cake. The sweetbreads' texture is perfect, having been cured overnight with salt and brown sugar to draw out some moisture.

Fresh oysters, often four or more varieties from the cold waters of Canada and the United States, start your meal. A seafood "tower" is perfect for a group to sample the finest from the sea, piled high with both raw and cooked crustaceans, oysters, and other shellfish. House-smoked salmon, tuna tartare, grilled octopus, steamed mussels, poached lobster, Gulf shrimp, crab, and diver scallops round out the bounty offered daily on both lunch and dinner menus.

In a funky twist, the reasonably priced wine list is a high-tech interactive touch pad, left at your table. Drop-down menus allow you to search for that perfect bottle by region, type, vintage, varietal, label, and bottle size. Scan through the thumbnail images and tap on one to open a page with all the details of your selection. Brasserie 19 also offers lists of wines by the glass and house beer offerings as well, so you can indulge in the perfect drink to go with your meal.

Asparagus & Beet Salad

SERVES 4–6

In a pinch, processed beets in jars can substitute, but fresh beets are superior. Consider using disposable gloves when working with the beets, as they can stain your hands. Frisée is also called curly endive and is related to escarole, a less bitter, broader-leaf variety of greens.

For the salad:

1 bunch asparagus, blanched, trimmed,
    cut into 1-inch pieces
1 orange, peeled, pith removed, divided
    into segments
1 fennel bulb, sliced very thin (use a mandolin,
    if possible)
1 head baby frisee, green tops removed,
    torn into small pieces
8 ounces baby arugula
1 cup celery leaves
1 gold beet, roasted, peeled, diced, cooled
1 red beet, roasted, peeled, diced, cooled

For the vinaigrette:

1 cup olive oil
1/3 cup white balsamic vinegar
1 shallot, peeled and minced
Salt and pepper

For the citrus-herb yogurt:

1 cup plain yogurt
Zest of 1 orange
½ tablespoon lemon juice
1 tablespoon minced chives

Toss the salad ingredients together, except for the diced red beets.

Whisk the olive oil with the balsamic vinegar and shallot. Season the vinaigrette with salt and pepper.

Toss the salad with vinaigrette. Adjust seasoning with salt and pepper.

Mix the yogurt with the orange zest, lemon juice, and chives.

Place a spoonful of yogurt mixture on each plate and top with portions of tossed salad. Scatter reserved red beets over salads and serve immediately.

SEARED DIVER SCALLOPS
WITH ROASTED FENNEL PURÉE

SERVES 4

"Large," "giant," and "jumbo" labels can be misleading when evaluating the size of an individual piece of seafood. To avoid this commercially, seafood is usually shown as an average number per pound. As an example 16 to 20 jumbo shrimp would average just less than 1 ounce per shrimp (16 ounces = 1 pound). One of the largest classifications, which is indicated for the scallops in this dish, is "U10," meaning under 10 pieces per pound.

2 fennel bulbs, fronds removed and reserved,
    bulbs sliced
4 garlic cloves, minced
2 tablespoons butter
1 cup cream
¼ cup olive oil
Pinch salt
Canola oil
8 jumbo scallops (size U10), patted dry

Combine sliced fennel bulbs, garlic, and butter in roasting pan, cover with foil, and roast at 400°F for 20 minutes.

Add the roasted fennel and the contents of the pan to a blender and purée with 1 cup cream. Reserve.

Blanch the reserved fennel fronds in boiling water for 1 minute. Immediately remove them to an ice bath. Drain and purée with olive oil and salt. Reserve the frond oil for service.

In a hot skillet add some canola oil to coat the bottom of the pan. Sear the scallops on one side until brown, about 1 minute. Turn and brown the other sides, about 1 minute.

To serve, spoon a portion of warm fennel purée on plate. Top with 2 seared scallops. Drizzle fennel frond oil over the plate to garnish. Field pea salad (see below) makes a nice accompaniment.

FIELD PEA SALAD

MAKES ABOUT 2½ CUPS

Field peas were brought to America from Africa during the slave trade days. The term includes Crowder peas, purple hull peas, black-eyed peas, and cream peas, to name a few.

1 pound shelled cream peas or purple hull peas
½ cup diced Fresno chile
½ cup diced red onion
¼ cup lemon juice
¼ cup extra-virgin olive oil
Salt and pepper

Cook the shelled peas in salted boiling water for 20 minutes or until just tender. Place them in an ice bath to cool. Drain.

Toss the cooled peas with the diced chile, onion, and lemon juice. Stir in the olive oil and adjust seasoning with salt and pepper. Refrigerate until needed.

ROMANO'S ITALIAN RESTAURANT
1528 West Gray Street

Just down the street from Brasserie 19 is a pizzeria reminiscent of a New York pizza shop, with an upscale atmosphere more in line with the River Oaks neighborhood of Houston. Its stone floors and warm wood tables are welcoming, as are the people behind the counter. The various pizzas, stromboli, meat rolls, and calzones are on display, and you walk up to the counter to order. In addition, you may select Sicilian-style (deep dish) or New York (thin crust), or an Italian sub with cold cuts or hot fillings such as veal parmigiana or meatball. The dough is exceptional, so whatever you choose will have a great base to start. The sauce is tasty and simple, and the toppings are piled high. You can buy by the slice or order a whole pie from 12-inch diameter to a large 20-inch. In addition to standard toppings such as sausage, pepperoni, and mushrooms, feta cheese, fresh basil, and spinach are available.

If pizza is not to your liking, there is an assortment of classic Italian dinners such as veal, chicken and eggplant parmagiana, spaghetti with meatballs, lasagna, and manicotti. A complete set of condiments, not often on the table outside of New York, include quality grated cheese, spicy crushed red pepper, oregano, and dried garlic.

DOLCE VITA
500 Westheimer Road

Next door to Indika is a special place to have pizza, in a beautiful old house with bead board ceilings, a large enclosed patio, and upstairs dining. The heart of this pizzeria is its ovens. Most pizzerias rely on commercial stainless steel gas or electric deck ovens. Rarely do you encounter an authentic wood oven. Many ovens reputed to be wood actually rely on gas or electricity with a small wood-burning section to provide "atmosphere" and a wood taste. This pizzeria has the real deal. Pizzas are baked from the heat of glowing coals constantly fed with logs. Not only does this impart the correct flavor, but it generates the high temperatures needed to duplicate the rustic ovens of Italy. The crust comes out charred in spots where the dough rises rapidly and on the bottom, in contact with the stone hearth. The cheese is fresh mozzarella rather than grated from a loaf, and the toppings offered are of the highest quality and not often encountered elsewhere, such as porchetta, speck, rapini, leeks, prosciutto, clams, pancetta, and arugula.

If you would rather sit back and enjoy some wine with little plates to snack on, Dolce Vita offers small plates of fish—salmon, octopus, calamari, and others— and cured meats such as mortadella, sopressata, and culatello. There are fried offerings of baby artichokes, pumpkin croquettes, and mozzarella, cheese plates and salads such as Caprese, arugula, and roasted tomatoes, and a variety of luscious pasta dishes.

STAR PIZZA
2111 Norfolk Street

Two blocks north of the 59 South Freeway off Shepherd is one of Houston's favorite pizza destinations. Star Pizza occupies a huge, two-story house that takes up almost an entire block and has a roadhouse atmosphere. Opened in 1976, it must be doing something right, as thirty-five years is quite a long time in the restaurant business. Star Pizza attracts an eclectic clientele of families, couples, and businesspeople at all hours of the day. While they offer a lunch buffet, many opt for a freshly made pizza with their favorite toppings. One of the most requested is Joe's pizza with spinach sautéed with garlic, and a close second is the rosemary and garlic grilled chicken pizza.

Many think that this is the place for deep-dish pizza in Houston, which they call Chicago style.

Regardless of style selected, Star offers over thirty-five toppings from which to choose, so anyone can build a pizza to their liking. The individual focaccia pizzas (8-inch) have great topping combinations such as the Portofino with kalamata olives, feta cheese, artichoke hearts, red onions, Roma tomatoes, basil, and olive oil. They also do pizza by the slice for a fast, light lunch. There are many large tables ready for parties of eight or more, and unlike many restaurants, they offer extra-large salads that can serve a dozen or more, so bring a crowd if you like.

Non-pizza diners will enjoy the cannelloni, lasagna, pasta with a selection of six sauces, or sandwiches, cold and hot.

BROTHER'S PIZZERIA
1029 Highway 6 North

This is one pizza worth the drive. Just north of I-10 on Highway 6, Brother's is not the most convenient pizzeria, but it is one of the best in or out of town. Its New York-style pizza has it all—quality dough, superior cheese, tasty toppings, and unobtrusive but essential sauce. The cheese alone sets this pie apart from the common delivery shops. Not just a glue for holding toppings onto the pizza, the mozzarella should have flavor, and here it contributes much to the overall experience, one overlooked much too often. At lunch they do a tremendous by-the-slice business, and the line begins to get long by 11:15 a.m. and lasts through the lunch rush.

A cadre of eight workers in the back is busy tossing the dough and shuttling pies around to bake them to a uniform golden brown. Despite potentially long lines, the slices come flying out of the back, where a bank of standard pizza deck ovens resides, with no shortcuts taken. Decor is simple with lots of autographs of cheerleaders, Miss Teen competitors, drag racers, and boxers covering the walls.

If you want several pizzas for a party, be prepared to drive, as Brother's does not deliver. This does not seem to deter as it is common to see patrons walk out with boxes stacked so high, they can barely peer over the top box to see the door. Hot subs, calzone, stromboli, baked ziti, lasagna, chicken or eggplant parmigiana, manicotti, ravioli, and spaghetti round out the non-pizza offerings.

BARRY'S PIZZA AND ITALIAN DINER
6003 Richmond Avenue

Barry's Pizza is set in a Texas log cabin, so don't expect red and white checkered tablecloths and Chianti bottles with dripping candle wax on the tables. It has that relaxed roadhouse feel to it with open spaces so you never feel crowded. Weather permitting, kick back on their covered deck and enjoy their ultimate appetizer platter of fried mushrooms, buffalo wings, mozzarella sticks, and fried ravioli with a cold beer or glass of wine. The style of hand-tossed pizza at Barry's is a bit different, in that the crust is neither very thin nor deep-dish style. The raised crust is due to their slow baking at a lower temperature than at many pizzerias. The result, in addition to the rising of the dough, is to produce a uniformly golden crust and bottom to the pizza. They do have a Sicilian deep-dish pizza if that is to your liking. You can build your own with more than thirty toppings or try one of their gourmet pizzas, such as the delicious white pizza with Alfredo sauce, grilled chicken, sautéed spinach, mushrooms, and Asiago cheese. In addition to pizza there are large salads, sub sandwiches, and Italian entrees such as spinach cannelloni, lasagna, and a tasty grilled chicken with homemade pesto, tossed together with penne pasta. They offer a kid's menu and, if you have any room left, New York cheesecake and Barry's Big Brownie for dessert.

CANOPY

MONTROSE
3939 MONTROSE BOULEVARD
(713) 528-6848
WWW.CANOPYHOUSTON.COM
CHEF: ELIZABETH BROOKS
OWNER: CLAIRE SMITH

You've been told to eat your vegetables. Canopy makes this easy as it incorporates flavorful veggies in copious amounts to accompany their dishes. This is not a vegan restaurant, but it does understand the necessity of a healthy diet. Canopy is tailored to the neighborhood in which it resides: Montrose is hip, progressive, and artsy. Canopy reflects this with a modernized 1950s style in its decor. Walls are reserved for local artists to display their works; the lofty ceiling houses a modern wood sculpture.

Owner Claire Smith prides herself on freshly baked goods, and everything is baked in-house, from the domed pastry plate offered for brunch with eight to ten hand-crafted miniature pastries (bear claws, Danish, croissants, strudel, and Bundt cakes) to the sweet potato English muffin supporting their interpretation of eggs Benedict: chipotle Hollandaise, wilted spinach, Canadian bacon, and a perfectly poached egg. Canopy houses the bakery that also serves their sister restaurant, Shade, and does some wholesale breads to neighboring restaurants. The dishes are not heavy on animal

protein, and can be augmented with lentils and wheat berries, disguised as a pilaf under a modest portion of grilled salmon, with grilled fennel and tomato chutney.

Unlike many vegetarian dishes, Chef Brooks makes sure you feel satisfied and content, while tossing in unexpected surprises to liven up a salad. Candied, preserved lemon wedges explode with flavor as you work your way through a salad of spring lettuces, edamame, cucumbers, and avocado dressed with sesame-lime vinaigrette. It's not all veggies and salads though, and the duck confit enchiladas with guajillo mole are not to be missed. One of the tastiest burgers in town is their Sabra Ranch Longhorn hamburger served on a house-baked challah bun.

ALMOND PEAR TART WITH BROWN BUTTER ICE CREAM

MAKES ONE 10-INCH TART (SERVES 6–8)

When baking the tart shell blind (without filling), several bakers' tricks can be used to keep the tart shell from sliding into the bottom of the pan, losing its beautiful shape. An easy method is to find an aluminum pie pan that just fits inside the rolled-out pastry. It can be removed about halfway through the baking process. Alternately line the pastry with foil and fill with raw rice or dry beans before baking blind.

For the dough:

8 ounces (1 cup) unsalted butter, at room temperature
¾ cup sugar
¼ cup almond paste
1 egg
¼ teaspoon pure vanilla extract
2²/₃ cups bread flour
Pinch baking soda
1 cup toasted chopped skinless almonds

For the filling:

6 ounces almond paste
3 ounces (6 tablespoons) softened unsalted butter
1½ tablespoons sugar
1 egg and 1 yolk
2 tablespoons cake flour

For the poached pears:

2 cups water
2 cups sugar
1 vanilla bean, split
2 star anise
2 bay leaves
2 allspice berries
6 Bosc pears (or other variety), peeled,
    halved, and cored
Brown butter ice cream (recipe follows), optional

Using an electric mixer, cream the butter with the sugar and almond paste until light and fluffy. Beat in the egg and vanilla.

Mix the flour, baking soda, and chopped almonds together and add to the butter mixture. Stir to form a smooth dough. Refrigerate until needed.

For the filling, beat the almond paste with the butter and sugar until smooth and light. Beat in the egg and yolk until uniform. Stir in the cake flour.

Mix the water, sugar, vanilla bean with its seeds scraped into the water, the anise, bay leaves, and allspice together. Heat this mixture to a simmer. Add the pears and cook 5 minutes or until just tender. Drain the pears, allow them to cool, and cut into ¼-inch-thick slices.

Roll the dough out to line a 10-inch removable-bottom tart pan. Thoroughly chill and bake blind 20 minutes at 350°F. Allow to cool.

Add the filling to the cooled shell and arrange the pear slices in a decorative manner. Bake an additional 20 to 30 minutes, until golden and the filling is set. Allow to cool before serving. A scoop of brown butter ice cream (recipe follows) would make an excellent addition.

Brown Butter Ice Cream

MAKES ½ GALLON

8 ounces (1 cup) unsalted butter
2½ cups whole milk
1½ cups heavy cream
1 vanilla bean, split
10 egg yolks
2 cups sugar
Pinch salt

In a heavy saucepan, melt the butter over low heat and allow to simmer until it just browns.

In a saucepan, combine the milk, cream, and vanilla bean, scraping the seeds into the milk. Heat to a simmer and stir in the browned butter.

Place the egg yolks in bowl and add the sugar. Whisk vigorously for about 30 seconds, until the sugar is incorporated and the yolks are pale yellow.

Whisk some of the hot milk mixture into the yolk mixture to temper the egg yolks. Add small portions of hot liquid, whisking constantly, until half of the liquid has been added. Pour the remaining milk mixture into the yolks and whisk to combine.

Strain the custard mixture into a heavy saucepan and cook over very low heat until it thickens, coating the back of a spoon, about 3 minutes. Do not allow the custard to boil at any time.

Strain the thickened custard and allow it to cool, placing plastic film over the surface to prevent a skin from forming. Refrigerate until thoroughly chilled.

Place the chilled custard into an ice-cream maker and freeze according to manufacturer's instructions.

Grilled Salmon with Wheat Berries & Lentils

SERVES 4

Wheat berries are the entire wheat kernel. Only the hull has been removed. It contains the bran, germ, and endosperm, making for a very nutritious food. They are quite chewy when cooked and do not require an overnight soaking, but do require thorough cooking. Steaming for about 1¼ hours or simmering for almost 2 hours is usually required.

For the salmon:

4 (6-ounce) salmon fillets
½ cup olive oil
Salt
¼ cup chopped fresh thyme, stems removed

¼ cup chopped Italian parsley
½ cup dry, unseasoned bread crumbs, such as panko
Salt and pepper
2–3 cups Wheat Berry and Lentil Pilaf (see page 30)
Tomato jam (see page 30)

For the pilaf (makes 5 cups):

½ cup finely diced red onion

1 medium carrot, peeled and finely diced

½ medium red bell pepper, finely diced

1 celery stalk, finely diced

6 tablespoons olive oil

2 cups cooked lentils (1 cup uncooked lentils makes 2 cups)

2 cups cooked wheat berries (1 cup uncooked wheat berries makes 2 cups)

¼ cup sliced green onions

½ cup chopped Italian parsley

Zest 1 lemon and its juice

Coarse salt

Freshly ground black pepper

For the tomato jam (makes about 1 gallon):

3 tablespoons extra-virgin olive oil

¼ teaspoon coriander seeds

6 star anise

¼ teaspoon cumin seeds

¼ teaspoon fennel seeds

12 garlic cloves, peeled and minced

1 (2-inch) slice fresh ginger, peeled and minced

4 (28-ounce) cans diced tomatoes in juice

1¼ cups red wine vinegar

¾ cup sugar

1½ teaspoons salt

¼ teaspoon cayenne

Heat a charcoal grill to medium high. Lightly oil the grill grates to keep the salmon from sticking.

Pat the salmon dry. Rub the fillets with olive oil and lightly season with salt. Place salmon on preheated grill and cook 4 to 5 minutes per side for medium.

Mix the thyme and parsley with the bread crumbs and lightly season with salt and pepper.

Press some of the bread crumb mixture onto each salmon fillet and place under a broiler until just browned.

To make the pilaf, sauté the onion, carrot, red bell pepper, and celery in olive oil over low heat for about 2 minutes, leaving the vegetables slightly crisp.

Add the cooked lentils and wheat berries. Toss to combine. Add the green onions and parsley.

Mix in the lemon zest and juice, and adjust seasoning with coarse salt and freshly ground pepper. Reserve, refrigerated, until needed.

Make the tomato jam by heating the oil in a 2- or 3-quart heavy saucepan over moderately high heat until hot but not smoking. Add coriander seeds. When the seeds begin to pop, add the star anise, cumin, and fennel. Stir and lower the heat to medium.

Add the garlic and ginger and cook 1 minute, being careful not to burn the garlic. Add the tomatoes with their juice, and the vinegar, sugar, salt, and cayenne. Bring the mixture to a boil.

Lower the heat and simmer uncovered, stirring occasionally, until thickened, about 2 hours. Lower the heat as necessary while the mixture reduces.

Transfer the tomato jam to a large bowl and allow to cool. Divide the jam into clean containers and refrigerate until needed.

Add portions of wheat berry and lentil pilaf to serving plates. Add ½ cup tomato jam on the side of each plate. Top the wheat berries and lentils with salmon fillets and serve immediately.

Ciao Bello

Galleria
5161 San Felipe Street
(713) 960-0333
www.ciaobellohouston.com
Chef: Bobby Matos
Owner: Tony Vallone

When Tony Vallone opens a new restaurant, it immediately gains the attention of Houstonians. Ciao Bello offers food of the same quality and care in preparation as you would find in Vallone's flagship restaurant, Tony's, but it's less formal, more relaxed, and family friendly. This soaring space in the Galleria area welcomes you and makes you feel relaxed and unrushed. The ceilings are two stories tall, and the wall of windows allows diffused light to warmly highlight the restrained decor. Splashes of color accent the dining room through fanciful paintings of pizza, vegetables, and fish. While informal, Jeff Vallone, Tony's son, is constantly (and unobtrusively) seeing to every detail of the food and the service, which is impeccable. But the restaurant is carefully overseen by Tony, making sure every dish is cooked to its fullest flavor and tweaking recipes to ensure compliance with authenticity and respect for the quality of ingredients he so carefully obtains.

The pastas are all house-made, and the Tagliarini Pomodoro is an example of how simple ingredients cooked with respect can elevate a dish to perfection. Sweet cherry tomatoes are roasted to intensify their flavor, and when the plate is set in front of you, the aroma of tomatoes fills your senses. A bit of garlic and extremely fine olive oil complete the dish. Seafood has always been a mainstay of Tony Vallone's restaurants, and the Gulf Flounder en Brodo is a signature dish of Ciao Bello. Each serving is a masterfully prepared 1-pound flounder, boned and hinge-cut to allow the tail to remain attached to the fillets. Garnishes include shrimp, calamari, littleneck clams, and mussels, all cooked perfectly, which is no easy task considering all have different cooking times to make them just right.

Occasionally a more sophisticated dish may slip into the menu, such as sumptuous braised beef cheeks on soft polenta, but there are family favorites such as spaghetti and meatballs (a secret family recipe), eggplant or chicken parmagiana and lasagna Bolognese. Fish lovers can be satisfied with the freshest sea bass, salmon, and snapper. Carnivores will love the New York strip with truffled potatoes, a prime filet, or veal with wild mushrooms. Desserts are luscious and presented on a cart, making it irresistible to leave without having one (to-go boxes are at the ready). Ciao Bello has a wonderful Sunday brunch menu if you cannot get enough of this wonderful place during the week.

TAGLIARINI POMODORO

SERVES 2

It's hard to find really sweet tomatoes these days, and chefs are relying more on the miniature varieties, such as cherry tomatoes. To intensify flavor, roasting brings out the sweetness and concentrates flavor by removing excess moisture.

¼ cup extra-virgin olive oil

2 tablespoons minced garlic

1 cup cherry tomatoes that have been roasted
   in the oven for 30 minutes at 350°F

1 cup pomodoro (imported tomato purée)

1 pound pasta cooked 90 percent
   (or freshly made)

6 torn basil leaves

Salt and pepper

Heat the oil in a large skillet over medium heat. Add the garlic and sauté briefly. Toss in the tomatoes and sauté 1 minute. Add the tomato purée and sauté 1 minute.

Drop the pasta into salted boiling water for 1 minute. Drain and add to the skillet. Toss briefly.

Add the basil, and adjust seasoning with salt and pepper. Serve immediately.

GULF FLOUNDER EN BRODO

SERVES 2

In a restaurant, presentation is very important, and the hinge cut of the flounder makes for a striking dish. The whole flounder is filleted, but the connection at the tail remains, leaving both fillets attached and more like a whole fish that has been boned and left intact. Feel free to use individual fillets when making this recipe.

¾ cup olive oil

1 red bell pepper, julienne

1 yellow pepper, julienne

3 garlic cloves, sliced thin

2 shallots, minced

1 fennel bulb, fronds removed, sliced thin

4 mussels

4 littleneck clams

2 cups white wine

2 ounces calamari, with tentacles

4 large shrimp

2 cups clam juice

2 lemons, thinly sliced

Pinch of saffron

2 small (1 pound each) flounders, "hinge cut,"
   leaving tail attached, boned and skinned

Salt and pepper

Heat ½ cup of the olive oil in a saucepan over medium heat. Add the bell peppers, garlic, shallots, and fennel. Sauté briefly to sweat the vegetables.

Add the mussels and clams. Pour in the wine and cover the pan. Cook 3 minutes or until the mussels and clams have just opened. Add the calamari and shrimp and cook 2 minutes over low heat, uncovered.

Remove the fish from the pan to a warm platter. Add the clam juice, lemon slices, and saffron. Simmer and reduce the volume of liquid by half.

While liquid is reducing, add the remaining ¼ cup olive oil to a large skillet over medium heat. Sear the flounder on both sides and cook until done, about 4 minutes.

When the liquid has reduced, return the shellfish to the pan and season the broth with salt and pepper.

Plate the flounder and top with shellfish and broth. Serve immediately.

CINQ

MONTROSE
3410 MONTROSE BOULEVARD
(713) 524-7999
WWW.LACOLOMBEDORHOUSTON.COM
CHEF: FRANCIS LECRIQUE
OWNER: STEVE ZIMMERMAN

Most hotel restaurants are added as an afterthought to serve their guests, and these restaurants are not usually thought of as a dining destination by the city's residents. Rarely do you find a restaurant that becomes a hotel, but La Colombe d'Or started as a fine dining restaurant that offered five suites for guests to stay over. Recently a hurricane damaged the roof of the historic building, and owner Steve Zimmerman turned this into an opportunity to refresh the restaurant and renamed it CINQ, a play on the five senses, the five suites in the hotel, and the five Cs of hospitality.

Born in Brooklyn, New York, and raised in New Orleans, Zimmerman moved to Houston in the '60s. Recognizing the potential of the less than lustrous Montrose district, he purchased the home of the Walter Fondren family, founders of Humble Oil, and turned it into the most romantic dining destination in Houston. He often traveled to France

to bring back understudies of the masters of French culinary arts, but with the recent updating of the roof and dining room, Zimmerman daringly brought in a young American chef from Louisiana. In order to not disappoint the established regular diners of thirty years, he divided the menu in half, keeping the most requested entrees on one side of the menu (Classics) and allowing his new chef, Francis Lecrique, free rein over modern American cuisine with international influence on the other side (New Ideas).

Chef Lecrique respects his ingredients and has orders from Zimmerman to not worry about cost when shopping the local markets, but to select the absolute best quality. Dishes such as watermelon salad with heirloom yellow tomatoes and goat cheese feta or pan-seared grouper with jalapeño polenta and avocado relish reflect this quality and Chef's ability to show thoughtful restraint usually reserved for the more aged and experienced. The truffled macaroni and cheese is not to be missed, nor are the braised short ribs with roasted eggplant purée.

Heirloom Yellow Tomato & Watermelon Salad

SERVES 4

Modern groceries have forced growers to ship perfectly formed, blemish-free, and easy-to-ship produce, leading to tasteless and uninspiring fruits and vegetables by making hybrids. The latest trend is to seek out tomatoes that are nonhybrid and can be produced from seed. Often twisted, wrinkled, and unattractive, these varieties are nonetheless packed with flavor.

1 bunch tarragon, leaves only

1 bunch chervil, leaves only

1 bunch Italian parsley, leaves only

1 shallot, peeled and finely minced

6 tablespoons rice wine vinegar

1 cup extra-virgin olive oil

Salt and pepper

4 vine-ripened heirloom yellow tomatoes, stems and cores removed

1 ripe seedless watermelon, rind removed and cut into 3 x 3-inch squares about 1 inch thick

Sea salt

6 ounces crumbled feta cheese

Place the herb leaves in a damp cloth and refrigerate until needed.

For the vinaigrette, mix the shallot with the rice vinegar. Slowly whisk in the olive oil. Season with salt and pepper. Refrigerate until needed.

Slice the tomatoes ¼ inch thick and add 3 slices per chilled salad plate. Lay 2 pieces of melon on the tomatoes and stack 2 more slices of tomato on top. Sprinkle with sea salt.

Scatter the herbs over each salad. Add portions of feta and finish with a drizzle of the rice wine vinaigrette (whisk vigorously before adding). Serve immediately.

Grouper with Jalapeño Grits
& Avocado Relish

SERVES 4

Grouper refers to a variety of fish, including sea bass. Chilean sea bass has become one of the most desirable eating fish, but is endangered and must be certified "MSC" (Marine Stewardship Council) to be served in restaurants. A good alternative would be black cod (sablefish) or Pacific halibut.

For the grits:

½ cup freshly squeezed lemon juice

1 shallot, peeled and minced

1/3 cup olive oil

10 jalapeño peppers, halved, seeds and membrane
   removed

1 pound cooked grits, warmed

½ cup heavy cream

½ cup grated Parmesan

Salt and pepper

For the avocado relish:

1 red bell pepper, seeded, membrane removed
   and finely diced

1 yellow bell pepper, seeded, membrane removed
   and finely diced

1 avocado, peeled, pitted, and diced

1 medium tomato, halved, seeds removed by
   squeezing, diced

4 (7-ounce) grouper fillets (or swordfish)

¼ cup olive oil

Add ¼ cup lemon juice, the minced shallot, olive oil, and jalapeño peppers to a blender. Pulse until uniform. Fold this into the warm grits. Add the cream and Parmesan, stirring to combine. Adjust seasoning with salt and pepper.

For the relish, place the red and yellow bell peppers in a food processor. Add the avocado and tomato and gently pulse to break down the avocado, leaving some texture to the relish. Stir in the remaining ¼ cup lemon juice and adjust seasoning with salt and pepper. Reserve, refrigerated, until needed.

Heat the oven to 500°F. Pat the fish fillets with a clean towel. Heat 2 (10-inch) skillets over medium-high heat. Add the olive oil to the pans.

Dust the grouper fillets with salt and add them to the pans. Sear the fillets until golden brown, about 1 minute on each side. Place the skillets in the oven and cook for 4 to 6 minutes, depending on thickness.

Place portions of the grits on serving plates. Add the grouper fillets and top with avocado relish. Serve immediately.

Damian's Cucina Italiana

Midtown
3011 Smith Street
(713) 522-0439
www.damians.com
Chef: Napoleon Palacios
Owners: Frankie Mandola and Joe Butera

Capturing Old World atmosphere, Damian's is a dining destination suitable for a romantic evening, a cozy dinner with friends, or a family affair. Established by Damian Mandola in the early '80s, it has been under the auspices of Joe (Bubba) Butera and Frankie Mandola for eighteen years and in the same Midtown location since inception. Service is impeccable and the food masterfully created and presented. Everyone involved works to make your dining experience notable, and you are welcomed as family when entering the door.

All pastas, breads, and desserts are made in-house, and this care for quality filters down to their carefully selected Italian wines. Their philosophy is that no one should have to drink marginal quality wine by the glass, and house wines are excellent. One nice throwback to service in the '70s is their tableside preparation of Caesar salad. Your server wheels to your table a cart with a large wooden bowl and all the accoutrements to make the salad, and prepares it in front of you. All other menu items come from the experienced kitchen (their head chef Napoeon Palacios has been there for over twenty years) to maintain uniformity.

First courses include antipasti of cold cuts and cheeses, prosciutto-wrapped asparagus, and delicate sweet potato ravioli in sage butter sauce. Entrees include veal piccata and marsala and a rolled pork tenderloin (*involuti*) stuffed with spinach, sun-dried tomatoes, and fontina cheese. A pasta dish not to be missed is the linguini gamberoni with black garlic, roasted cherry tomatoes, and garlicky shrimp, all drizzled in fine olive oil. Other pasta dishes come with tiger shrimp and lump crab in a rosa sauce, Bolognese-sauced spaghetti, linguini with clams in a white wine sauce, and a wonderful lasagna with ground veal. Fresh fish and succulent poultry round out the offerings. An overly generous portion of tiramisu will fill in any space left after your meal, and the lemon tart seems perfect with a properly made espresso.

Linguine alla Gamberoni

SERVES 2

Used for ages in Asian medicine, black garlic is garlic that has undergone a month-long fermentation process without additives. Its flavor resembles molasses and garlic combined and its texture is jelly-like. It is becoming quite popular among top chefs. To substitute used roasted garlic cloves mixed with a bit of molasses.

1 cup halved cherry tomatoes
6 jumbo shrimp (size 16/20), peeled and deveined
2 tablespoons extra-virgin olive oil
2 tablespoons black garlic, if available (see above)
8 ounces dry linguine, cooked 90 percent
3 basil leaves, chiffonade
Salt and pepper

Preheat the oven to 350°F. Roast the cherry tomato halves, cut side up, in the preheated oven for 10 minutes, or until dried and shriveled, but still soft and pliable.

Bring 2 quarts of salted water to a boil.

In a large skillet sauté the shrimp in 2 tablespoons olive oil over medium heat 1 minute. Add the garlic and continue to sauté the shrimp.

Add the precooked linguine to the boiling water and cook 1 minute until done. Drain.

Add the basil and cherry tomatoes to the shrimp and adjust seasoning with salt and pepper.

Toss the linguine with the shrimp in the skillet and serve immediately, carefully arranging the shrimp around each plate.

Spaghetti alla Carbonara

SERVES 2

The original recipe for carbonara is to use whole raw eggs that are stirred into hot pasta off heat. Restaurants must be careful to avoid raw eggs, a component of potential food-borne illness (salmonella). This method of using egg yolks and cream as a thickener is safer and quite delicious.

¼ cup olive oil
¼ cup diced pancetta
2 tablespoons minced green onion
2 teaspoons minced garlic
½ cup heavy cream

2 egg yolks
2 ounces grated Parmesan
8 ounces dry spaghetti, cooked 90 percent
Salt and pepper

In a medium-size skillet heat the olive oil over low heat. Add the pancetta and sauté until it begins to brown. Add the green onion and garlic and sauté 2 minutes. The pancetta should be crisp.

Bring 2 quarts of salted water to a boil.

Add the heavy cream to the pancetta mixture and bring to a simmer.

Whisk the egg yolks with the Parmesan.

Add the precooked spaghetti to the boiling water and cook 1 minute. Drain and add to the pancetta cream mixture.

Stir in the egg-Parmesan mixture and cook 1 minute over low heat. Adjust seasoning with salt and pepper.

Veal Piccata

SERVES 2

The best veal to use for cuts called scallopini, scallops, or escalopes, such as in the recipe below, come from the leg and are sliced very thin as needed, from the hind saddle. This cut can be prohibitively expensive, so many use the shoulder to take slices, which are pounded thin with a kitchen mallet.

Salt and fresh ground pepper
6 slices (12 ounces) veal, cut from shoulder or leg
Flour to dredge
1/3 cup clarified butter
1/3 cup dry white wine
1/3 cup veal or chicken stock
1/3 cup fresh lemon juice
3 ounces (6 tablespoons) cold butter
1 tablespoon chopped Italian parsley

Salt and pepper the veal slices. Dredge them in flour.

Heat the clarified butter in a skillet over medium-high heat and add the veal slices. Brown both sides, about 1 minute per side. Transfer the cooked veal to a warm platter.

Pour off half the fat from the pan and return the pan to the heat.

Add the wine, stock, lemon juice, and any juices that have accumulated on the veal platter. Reduce, scraping up any bits from the bottom of the pan.

Swirl in the cold butter over very low heat. When the butter has emulsified the sauce, toss in the parsley. Add the veal just to warm it. Adjust seasoning with salt and pepper and serve immediately.

D'Amico's Italian Market Cafe

Rice Village
5510 Morningside Drive
(713) 526-3400
The Heights
2802 White Oak Drive, #500
(713) 868-3400
www.damico-cafe.com
Chef/Owner: Nash D'Amico

A slice of Little Italy came to Rice Village in 1996. Nash D'Amico, a Houston restaurateur of thirty years and cousin of Tony and Damian Mandola, opened this combination restaurant, market, and deli, and it has been bustling day and night from the moment it opened its doors. While customers shop for imported olive oils, cheeses, meats, and pastas up front, in back diners savor delicious northern Italian and southern Sicilian specialties from its immaculate kitchen.

The handmade pastas served in back can be purchased up front to take home and cook yourself, but why would you when you can sit and be served by experienced waiters, and allow the chefs to create delectable sauces for your enjoyment (just waiting to be mopped up with the luscious homemade table bread)? The crawfish ravioli is their most popular pasta, combining the best of the Gulf with Italian know-how. Plump bundles of fresh pasta are stuffed with crawfish tails, ricotta and Romano cheeses, and topped with a tomato-cream sauce packed with additional crawfish tails. The wild mushroom and walnut tortellini starts with fresh black pepper pasta and a stuffing of wild mushrooms, walnuts, and cheeses, and are then topped with a rich lemon butter sauce, laced with slices of wild mushrooms. Other pasta offerings include linguini diavolo loaded with seafood in a spicy tomato sauce, and a smoky spaghetti a la carbonara with pancetta.

A house specialty not to be missed is the chicken braciolentini, a boneless chicken breast stuffed with Italian sausage, ricotta, spinach, and basil and then glazed with brown butter and lemon. For diners looking for a vegetarian offering, the artichoke casserole served with sautéed spinach and garden veggies is big on flavor. Fish lovers should not pass up the snapper fillet, which is lightly battered, perfectly cooked, and topped with lump crabmeat and finished with a spicy lemon sauce. Traditionalists will appreciate spaghetti and meatballs, meat lasagna, cheese ravioli, and fettuccini Alfredo. Sliced meats from the deli make up a terrific antipasto plate. Save room for house-made tiramisu or a cannoli, if possible.

SNAPPER D'AMICO

SERVES 2

Fishing for Gulf red snapper is highly regulated to protect the species and to ensure an adequate supply for the table. Each year the commercial quota is set (3.66 million pounds in 2011) as are limits for the recreational angler. Gulf snapper fillets are a very popular menu item in many Texas restaurants.

¼ cup olive oil
2 (8-ounce) Gulf snapper fillets
½ cup flour
2 eggs, whisked
4 ounces (½ cup) unsalted butter
¼ teaspoon minced garlic
6 fluid ounces white wine
¼ cup clam juice
Pinch of salt
Pinch of freshly ground black pepper
Pinch of red pepper flakes
1 tablespoon lemon juice
3 ounces lump crabmeat, picked over for bits of shell
Pinch of fresh parsley

Heat oven to 350°F. Heat olive oil in a large sauté pan over medium heat. Dredge fish fillets in flour and then dip in beaten egg.

When the oil is hot, place the coated fillets in the sauté pan and brown on both sides. Place the pan in the oven for about 10 minutes or until the fish just flakes and is barely opaque throughout.

In a separate sauté pan over medium heat, combine half the butter, the garlic, white wine, clam juice, salt, pepper, and red pepper flakes. Raise the heat to high and add the remaining butter and lemon juice and reduce mixture by one-third.

When reduced, turn off the heat to the sauce and add the crabmeat. Swirl to combine. Place the snapper fillets on platter and pour the sauce over. Garnish with fresh parsley and serve immediately.

Gigi's Asian Bistro and Dumpling Bar

Galleria
5085 Westheimer Road, #B2515
(713) 629-8889
www.gigisasianbistro.com
Chef/Owner: Gigi Huang

The Galleria in Houston is the largest mall in Texas and seventh largest in the United States. Inside it looks like many malls across America, and if you were not paying attention, you would walk by Gigi's Asian Bistro and Dumpling Bar and not give it another thought. This would be a terrible mistake.

Its unassuming entrance leads into an explosion of cherry blossoms hanging from the ceiling of the main dining room. Suddenly you are transported from a mall into a fabulous dining space that seems miles from any retail outlet. It is truly an experience to behold. At the far end of this room is the "alley," with private dining tables and hanging fabrics across from the long kitchen, a secret passage that has the feeling of a typical alleyway somewhere in Southeast Asia. Continue farther and discover the Dumpling Bar, a great place to "graze" and have a refreshing beverage.

This pan-Asian restaurant is the brainchild of Gigi Huang, no stranger to the hospitality industry. Her father owned Hunan Restaurant, which had been a dining tradition in Houston for over thirty years. The menu offers a broad look into the cuisines of the Pacific Rim, a thoughtful mix of Thai, Chinese, Vietnamese, and Indonesian recipes brought to life by former Chef Junnajet Hurapan. He cleverly layers flavors, so that what lingers on the palate is not the first taste experience. Heavenly Beef is a fine example. Oven-dried and marinated sirloin is fork tender and concentrated in flavor. The finish is toasted coriander seed, an unexpected and delightful ending. Textures play on richness with the edamame dumplings. Delicate rice wrappers contain a purée of garlicky soy beans; their consistency is surprisingly creamy and unctuous. Other expertly prepared dumplings include *shu mai*, with delicate crabmeat replacing the anticipated pork. To add a bit of zing to the dumplings, Gigi's offers a platter of roasted Thai chiles, red chile dipping sauce, and spicy fish sauce on the side.

The crispy fillet whole fish seems a contradiction in name, but the fillets have been carefully laid out on the plate, maintaining the look of the whole fish, gracefully bending across the platter as though it was swimming toward you. The pad Thai is some of the best you will find anywhere, and the green curry chicken is rich in coconut milk, which takes the edge off the heat of Thai green curry paste. Japanese eggplant goes perfectly with the curry, and long beans add a textural crunch to this smooth-on-the-palate dish.

STEAMED SHRIMP & CRAB DUMPLINGS

MAKES 24 (4–6 SERVINGS)

Dumpling wrappers or skins can be found in most Asian markets and should not be confused with egg roll wrappers. Homemade are best and are not difficult to make.

10 ounces raw shrimp, peeled, deveined, and minced
    or ground
10 ounces crabmeat, picked over, finely chopped
3 ounces water chestnuts, drained and finely diced
2 teaspoons chopped scallions
1 tablespoon roasted garlic paste
2 tablespoons soy sauce
1 teaspoon white pepper
1 egg
1 tablespoon chopped cilantro
24 prepared round wonton/dumpling wrappers
    (or homemade)
¼ cup soy sauce
¼ cup orange juice
¼ cup lemon juice
¼ cup lime juice
¼ cup sugar

Combine the shrimp, crab, water chestnuts, scallions, garlic, soy sauce, and pepper in a bowl. Mix until well combined (an electric mixer may be used).

Place 1 tablespoon filling into the center of each wrapper. Twist the top to form a purse with a pleated edge, leaving a little of the filling exposed. Repeat until all wrappers are used.

Place the dumplings in a large steamer (or individual-serving steamers) and steam 10 minutes.

Prepare the dipping sauce by combining the soy sauce and orange, lemon, and lime juices with the sugar. This can be made 1 day in advance.

HUNAN GREEN BEANS

SERVES 4

For an authentic touch to this dish, use long beans, found in Asian markets. Also known as yardlong beans, they are not really a bean, but a vine.

1 tablespoon peanut oil
1 teaspoon grated ginger
1 teaspoon minced garlic
½ teaspoon ground hot chile
1 tablespoon fermented black beans
2 tablespoons mushroom soy sauce
½ teaspoon white pepper
1 pound green beans, ends trimmed,
    french cut into 1-inch segments

Heat the oil in a large skillet or wok over high heat. Add the ginger, garlic, ground chile, and fermented black beans. Stir 1 minute.

Stir in the mushroom soy sauce and white pepper. Add the green beans and stir-fry 1 to 2 minutes. The beans should be cooked but still crisp.

SHAKING BEEF WITH CHILE LIME VINAIGRETTE

SERVES 4

Shaking beef, a Vietnamese specialty, gets its name from the method of preparation. It is shaken constantly in a wok over ferociously high heat to avoid burning, but seared to perfection.

For the vinaigrette:

3 fresh Thai chiles, minced
¼ cup fresh lime juice
½ cup fish sauce (nuoc mam)
2 tablespoons palm sugar
2 teaspoons chopped cilantro
½ teaspoon chopped garlic

For the beef:

1½ pounds filet mignon, cut into 1-inch cubes
2 tablespoons peanut oil
½ teaspoon hot chile powder
1 medium red onion, thinly sliced
1 bunch watercress

For the vinaigrette, mix the Thai chiles, lime juice, fish sauce, palm sugar, chopped cilantro, and chopped garlic. Refrigerate until needed.

Sear the filet mignon cubes over high heat in the oil, adding the chile powder and onions after 1 minute. Cook an additional minute or two over high heat until medium rare or to desired doneness.

Add watercress to each serving plate. Top with beef and drizzle with chile-lime vinaigrette. Serve immediately.

KHUN KAY
1209 Montrose Boulevard

Thirty years ago it was difficult to have a strictly Thai menu in an Asian restaurant. Many Thai restaurateurs felt that offering a Chinese menu with some Thai dishes was the way to ensure steady business. Supatra Yooto and Kay Soodjai opened the Golden Room in 1982 with this philosophy in mind but steadily replaced the Chinese offerings with more and more authentic and creative Thai dishes. The restaurant became a landmark for Thai cuisine, but by 1998 the almost one-hundred-year-old house was in need of too much repair to be practical, so they razed the building and built new at the same location. Renamed Khun (Madame) Kay, this strictly Thai restaurant is brighter and more casual, forgoing waiters and

tablecloths. Guests walk up to the counter to order, and the food is brought out to the table you select.

The menu has traditional and expected Thai favorites such as pad Thai and pat see ew noodles, ka prow stir-fry with basil, tom ka and tom yum soups, and red, green, yellow, Massaman and Panang curries. Most dishes can be ordered with your favorite meat—pork, beef, chicken, or fish, squid, or shrimp. Everything is excellent, so order whatever strikes your fancy. The intensity of heat can be adjusted to your liking from mild to incendiary. Their creativity comes to light when it's time for dessert, usually thought of as a plate of mango and sticky rice with coconut cream. At Khun Kay, the mango is panko-coated and deep-fried and is accompanied by a scoop of coconut ice cream, a uniquely Khun Kay creation. In addition to the wonderful food, prices are remarkably reasonable, making this a must for Thai food aficionados.

HONG KONG DIM SUM
9889 Bellaire Boulevard, #110

The unassuming storefront of HK Dim Sum is the gateway to some of the tastiest dumplings to be found anywhere. The dining room is narrow and seats about 50 persons, unlike many dim sum houses around the world, which can seat more than 300 patrons at a time. Soy sauce, chile oil, and red vinegar are the table condiments, and when mixed, they make an ideal dipping sauce for the various dumplings, buns, and cakes.

The menu is divided into categories, and the steamed and pan-fried dim sum take center stage for the dumpling aficionado. Whether steamed or pan-fried, the dumpling skins are handmade and perfectly cooked when served. The pan-fried pork dumplings are outstanding, with a rich, meaty filling that has just a hint of sweetness. The pan-fried turnip cake is delicate and tastes of freshly grated turnips. Try the pan-fried stuffed tofu, deep-fried taro puff, or crispy shrimp roll before heading to the steamed portion of the menu.

Steamed dumplings have a translucent rice skin that subtly reveals its filling. The steamed seafood dumplings are exquisite as are the mixed meat, shrimp, and shrimp and pork. Bean curd sheet is filled with meat, rolled, steamed, and sliced into bite-size treats.

Non-dumpling offerings include steamed chicken feet, steamed sticky rice with meat in lotus leaf, and steamed buns filled with roast pork, red bean paste, or a mushroom/chicken combination. HK Dim Sum also serves tasty noodle bowls and soups.

SAIGON PADOLAC
9600 Bellaire Boulevard, Suite 119

This popular Vietnamese restaurant is expansive, seating about 200 guests in one large dining room. The service is attentive, and the food is fresh and subtly flavored. A huge salad plate is set out with traditional vegetables and herbs. A nice treat is that the cut vegetables have been marinated, and there are some uniquely Vietnamese greens added to the salad plate in addition to the expected lettuce, cilantro, parsley, bean sprouts, and basil.

With beef as the specialty of the house, dipping sauces include *mam nem*, a pineapple and anchovy sauce, in addition to the ubiquitous seasoned fish sauce *nuoc cham*. Vietnamese eggrolls, small by comparison to Chinese eggrolls, are very crisp and have a smooth filling. *Bahn xeo*, an enormous stuffed pancake, is filled with whole shrimp, slices of rich pork, and brimming with vegetables. A house specialty is beef served seven ways, a seven-course dinner including chopped beef rolled in Hawaiian ti leaf and charcoal grilled, beef noodle soup, beef meatballs, tenderloin fondue, char-grilled beef sausages, and marinated slices of beef over coals.

The extensive menu includes pho and bun as well as charcoal-grilled chicken and pork. Desserts can be mysterious and for the adventurous, such as durian milk shake or black grass jelly.

BANANA LEAF
9889 Bellaire Boulevard, #311

Tucked into the very back of the center that houses HK Dim Sum is a splendid Malaysian restaurant, serving classics of Malaysian cuisine in a small, modern space. The monitors on the walls flash photographs of the menu, making you hungrier than when you entered and willing to try some of these classics.

A good way to start the meal and to introduce your palate to the Malaysian style of cooking would be *rojak*, a sautéed fruit salad that is as much savory as sweet, owing to Malaysian use of fermented shrimp paste (*trassi*). This condiment forms the backbone of many of their dishes and can be quite strong if not used sparingly. Luckily the chefs understand the American palate and show restraint. As used at Banana Leaf, it provides richness and gives body to the dishes and is in no way off-putting.

Another classic is Hainanese chicken with rice. The chicken is steamed and served at room temperature. Steaming the whole chicken leaves the meat especially tender and juicy, and it is served with special soy dipping sauce and a basket of golden-colored rice that has been cooked in chicken stock. Beef rendang is another dish not to be missed when formulating a Malaysian meal. Slices of lean beef are simmered in a sauce perfumed with cinnamon, cloves, and lemongrass, and spiced with chiles. Coconut milk is the base for the sauce and forms a thick curry when finished.

Other menu offerings include *roti*, Indian pancakes or flatbreads that are filled and meant for dipping into assorted curries. Their noodle soups are excellent as are the rice dishes. If you are adventurous and like fish, try the fish head casserole, either in a coconut curry sauce or a sour sauce with eggplant and tomato.

ASIA MARKET
1010 West Cavalcade Street, Unit D

Just east of the busy intersection of 20th Street, West Main, and Studewood resides a modest grocery storefront housing one of the best Thai restaurants in the city—and a favorite of chefs. The food is authentic, intense, and spicy (which can be varied to suit your heat index). Mainly a small Thai grocery, one of the lanes has been removed and about ten small tables that each seat two persons have been added. You will definitely want to get there early, as the twenty or so seats fill fast. If you already are a fan of Thai cuisine, do not hesitate to order your favorite dish. You will see, in addition to standards such as pad Thai, pad woon sen, tom ka, and tom yum, soups such as boat noodle soup, which is fashioned in the same manner as on the floating boats that line the waters of Bangkok. The stock is rich and beefy; the noodles are authentic, as are the properly prepared meatballs, which are pounded rather than ground, to supply a unique texture and grain.

A tasty *laab* salad, in beef, pork, or chicken, comes as an overly generous serving of chopped meat, flavored with roasted rice powder, fish sauce, chiles, mint, and cilantro. The yum nur and nam tok beef salads are fresh and hearty, and the papaya salad is incendiary and refreshing. The curries are delicious, and the green curry with Thai eggplant is wonderful and can be prepared with red curry as well. Other curries include Massaman (yellow), Karee, and Panang. The fish cakes, listed under Specials

(*Tod Man Pla*) have just the right texture and make a great appetizer. The focus is on the food at Asia Market, so grab your own utensils, water, and tea from the service table, and tear off napkins from the rolls of paper towels scattered around the dining area.

FUNG'S KITCHEN
7320 Southwest Freeway

It may be cliché to state that to get great Chinese food, you should eat at a restaurant with mostly Chinese clientele, but it is often true. This dining room is cavernous with private rooms off to the sides. Rather than be part of a strip center, Fung's Kitchen *is* the strip center and is set up to cater parties of all sizes. The menu has a separate section for parties of ten with fixed menus from which to choose, each having ten menu items and special beverages included. The standard menu has not been Americanized—it offers soups such as fish maw with crab or the $150 bird's nest soup, appetizers of duck tongues (done two ways) or sesame jelly fish, entrees like abalone with dried shrimp and chives or sizzling wild boar tenderloin with house special sauce.

The menu features crab done almost twenty different ways, and tanks are filled with live crabs in circulating chilled water. Here is the place to order abalone, squid, conch, lobster, and sea cucumber, all done to perfection and handled with utmost care. Dim sum is served every day, and you may select from ninety-nine offerings in categories such as steam pastries, vegetarian, pan fried, rice noodle rice soup, baked, and supreme dishes. Throughout the day a dim sum cart with traditional desserts such as custard cups and steamed buns filled with sweet bean paste passes through the dining room to tantalize you.

Haven

Upper Kirby/River Oaks
2502 Algerian Way
(713) 581-6101
www.havenhouston.com
Chef/Owner: Randy Evans

Diffused light pours in from the large windows, exposing an attractive, open-air dining room. The tasteful decor is modern without being industrial. At the crossroads of Upper Kirby and River Oaks, this restaurant was built from the ground up to serve both its neighborhoods and all who desire the finest in local ingredients combined with big flavor and familiar food.

This is truly a "farm to table" restaurant, and the fare is Texan by nature, including all of the tasty influences of Mexico and Louisiana, as well as that of German and Czech settlers. Whenever possible the ingredients are locally sourced, and these sources are proudly listed at the bottom of each menu, as well as being italicized within each dish's menu description. Chef and owner Randy Evans highlights the freshness of ingredients by the subtitle of the restaurant, "A Seasonal Kitchen," and indicates vegetarian dishes with a small herb icon. Even the eggs are sourced locally and are spotlighted in a popular appetizer of free-range deviled eggs, with house-made bread-n-butter pickle relish and a dash of jalapeño. A playful take on fried shrimp is their State Fair–inspired shrimp corn dog appetizer with a remoulade made from Tabasco sauce mash and served with a mini-glass of lemonade. Okra fans will love the grilled okra and pickled okra duo topped with a spicy Avery Island dressing. Liver aficionados will applaud the fried chicken livers atop a mini-buttermilk biscuit, covered with cream gravy and chunks of house-made Andouille sausage.

Salads are wonderful, especially the arugula and fresh peach with candied pecans and goat cheese crostini. Torn greens with cubes of fried green tomatoes and topped with Veldhuizen cheddar makes a perfect Texas/Southern statement. Wild boar chili con carne is spicy and richly loaded with coarsely ground Texas-grown boar. Sliders of slowly smoked (thirty hours over pecan wood) pulled pork are topped with cilantro cider slaw and Texas 1015 onions. Those that appreciate the true flavor of Gulf shrimp will enjoy the wild, head-on variety served with shrimp boudin and cheesy grits, sucking on the separated heads to extract the most concentrated of shrimp essence imaginable. Great desserts include fresh peach sorbet topped with an ambrosia of fruit in season, homemade ice creams, coconut *tres leches* garnished with toasted marshmallow, and refrigerator chocolate ice box pie.

COUNTRY-FRIED CHICKEN LIVERS ON BISCUITS & GRAVY

SERVES 4

Many people do not like liver because they had it overcooked when first prepared for them. Liver takes on a very bitter and metallic flavor when overcooked, so be careful to cook all liver medium, with a blush of pink in the center.

For the chicken livers:

16 chicken livers, deveined
2 cups buttermilk
2 tablespoons Crystal brand hot sauce
Salt and pepper
2 cups all-purpose flour mixed with 1 teaspoon garlic
    powder and 1 teaspoon onion powder

For the biscuits and Andouille sausage gravy:

1 cup all-purpose flour
½ tablespoon baking powder
¼ teaspoon baking soda
¼ teaspoon salt
2 tablespoons cold shortening
½ cup cold buttermilk
8 ounces Andouille sausage, cut into small dice
¼ cup all-purpose flour
2⅓ cups warm milk
Salt and black pepper
Italian parsley leaves for garnish

Combine the livers, buttermilk, and hot sauce in a nonreactive bowl and refrigerate 4 hours or overnight.

Remove the livers from the buttermilk mixture and allow to drain. Season with salt and pepper. Dredge the livers in seasoned flour and deep-fry at 350°F until livers float to the top and are cooked through, about 3 minutes.

Remove the livers from the fryer and place on a wire rack to drain. Sprinkle with salt and pepper.

For the biscuits, in a small mixing bowl combine the flour, baking powder, baking soda, and salt. Cut in the shortening with a pastry knife or fork. Add the buttermilk and mix until just combined. The mixture should be quite coarse and barely holding together.

Preheat the oven to 325°F. Roll (or pat) the dough out ½ inch thick on a floured surface. Cut out biscuits using a 2-inch cutter. Place on a baking sheet. Bake in the preheated oven for 20 minutes. Cool on a wire rack.

For the gravy, cook the sausage in a skillet over medium heat for 5 minutes, rendering the fat. Remove the sausage, leaving the fat in the pan.

Whisk the flour into the fat in the pan, forming a smooth paste. Cook, whisking constantly, about 1 minute. Slowly whisk in the milk, and then cook, whisking constantly, 5 to 7 minutes or until thickened. Stir in sausage and cook over low heat for 5 minutes. Adjust seasoning with salt and pepper.

To serve, split the biscuits in half and toast under a broiler for 1 minute. Spoon some gravy on each plate and place 4 toasted biscuit halves on the gravy. Spoon more gravy over the biscuits.

Place a fried liver on each smothered biscuit half and top each with a fresh parsley leaf.

GULF SHRIMP CORN DOGS WITH TABASCO MASH REMOULADE

SERVES 6

The technique for forming a uniform coating around a corn dog is to slowly twirl it by the stick as you gently submerge the corn dog into the hot oil and then release it. Do not drop them directly into the oil.

For the corn dogs:

12 jumbo (size 16/20) shrimp, peeled and deveined
12 (6-inch) wooden skewers
Coarse salt and black pepper to taste
Flour for dredging
3 cups cornmeal
1½ cups flour
1¼ teaspoons baking soda
¾ teaspoon salt
1 tablespoon Texas honey
1½ cups buttermilk
1¼ cups water
1 egg

For the Tabasco remoulade sauce (makes 1½ cups):

¼ cup finely chopped green onions
2 tablespoons finely chopped celery
2 tablespoons finely chopped parsley
2 tablespoons ketchup
2 tablespoons horseradish mixed with a dash of
    Tabasco sauce (or Tabasco mash if available)
2 tablespoons Creole mustard
1 tablespoon prepared yellow mustard
1 tablespoon white vinegar
2 teaspoons lemon juice
¾ teaspoon paprika
1 egg
1 garlic clove, minced
⅛ teaspoon salt
6 tablespoons vegetable oil

Skewer the shrimp lengthwise starting at the tail end. Season with salt and pepper and then dredge the shrimp in flour.

Prepare the batter by mixing the cornmeal, flour, baking soda, and salt together.

Mix the honey with the buttermilk and water. Whisk in the egg. Stir in the dry ingredients to form a smooth batter. Allow to stand 5 minutes.

Roll the skewered shrimp in the batter and deep-fry at 350°F until golden brown.

For the Tabasco mash or sauce, place all the ingredients except for the oil in a blender or food processor. Mix at high speed until well blended.

While processing, gradually add the oil in a slow, steady stream. The sauce will thicken to a creamy consistency. Adjust spice with additional Tabasco mash if desired.

Store, covered, in the refrigerator. The sauce can be held, refrigerated, up to 1 week.

Serve 2 shrimp with 2 ounces Tabasco mash dipping sauce. For a unique presentation serve a miniature glass of lemonade on the side.

Hubbell and Hudson Bistro

The Woodlands
24 Waterway Avenue, Suite 125
(281) 203-5641
www.hubbellandhudson.com/bistro
Chef: Austin Simmons

Classically contemporary in its interior design, the Bistro invites you to relax and enjoy your meal. Warm tones and subdued lighting lend an air of comfort with large windows screened from the sun and the bustle of the street. The Bistro is part of a more ambitious food destination than just a restaurant. Hubbell and Hudson is an upscale market, a cooking school, and a catering facility all in one, designed to be this way from inception. For a chef this is an extraordinary situation. Your pantry is an entire food market, with the purchasing power and connections to get almost anything made anywhere. And you certainly don't worry about running out of some ingredient when the food store is just an open door away.

The menu has something for every mood. Starters include foie gras with apple-fig compote, black truffle risotto, seared ahi tuna, Texas quail, and a fantastic cheese board. One unique aspect of the menu is a mix-and-match section where you choose a meat such as rib-eye or tenderloin, a rub such as Jamaican jerk or Cajun, and a sauce to accompany, such as béarnaise, barbecue, or Stilton demi-glace. There is a fantastic swordfish dish on the menu, cooked perfectly, resting on a bed of creamy polenta, along with snapper, salmon, and scallops. The pork shank is fork-tender and sumptuous.

7-Spice Braised Pork Shanks

SERVES 4

Chefs are discovering more and more parts of the pig to cook. These cuts, such as pork belly, jowls, and shanks, have always been the cheapest cuts, which poor people have relied on for years to fill their cooking pots. Prices are soaring now that they have been "discovered."

For the shanks:

4 (1-pound) pork shanks
½ tablespoon coarse salt
½ tablespoon black pepper
2 tablespoons herbes de Provence
½ cup canola oil
1¼ cups Chablis

½ cup soy sauce
½ cup veal stock
1 cup diced white onions
1 tablespoon chopped thyme
¼ cup minced garlic
1 tablespoon light brown sugar
1 tablespoon chipotle powder

1 tablespoon ground cumin

1 tablespoon madras curry

1 tablespoon ground ginger

1 tablespoon ground nutmeg

⅓ cup tomato paste

For the risotto:

10 ounces (1¼ cups) butter

1 teaspoon extra-virgin olive oil

2 tablespoons minced shallots

1 teaspoon minced garlic

1 tablespoon chopped fresh thyme

4 ounces Arborio rice

3 tablespoons sweet vermouth

1½ tablespoons turmeric

½ tablespoon saffron threads

2 cups simmering chicken stock

¼ cup grated Parmesan

Coarse salt

White pepper

Season the pork shanks with salt, pepper, and herbes de Provence.

Heat the oil in a large pot and brown the shanks on all sides. Add the Chablis to deglaze the pan. Cook over medium heat to reduce liquid by half.

Add the soy sauce and veal stock. Simmer 2 minutes. Add the onions, thyme, garlic, and brown sugar. Simmer 2 minutes. Add the remaining ingredients and cook 2 minutes.

Place the shanks in a roasting pan. Strain the cooking liquid over the shanks and cover the pan tightly with foil.

Bake at 350°F for 2 hours or until "falling off the bone" tender.

For the risotto, heat 2 ounces (¼ cup) of the butter and the olive oil in a deep sauté pan over medium heat. Add the shallots, garlic, and thyme and sauté until the onions are translucent.

Add the rice and sauté until the grains are translucent, about 5 minutes. Add the vermouth and cook until almost dry. Stir in the turmeric and saffron.

Add simmering chicken stock, 2 fluid-ounce ladles at a time, stirring constantly, until each ladle is absorbed before adding the next ladle. Repeat, constantly stirring, until the rice is cooked and has turned creamy from releasing the starch.

Stir in the remaining 8 ounces of butter and the Parmesan. Adjust seasoning with salt and pepper.

Place each pork shank on some of the saffron risotto and drizzle with pan juices. Serve immediately.

Seared Swordfish with Mushroom Ragout on Truffled Polenta

SERVES 4

If overcooked, swordfish is dry and tough in texture. As an extremely firm-flesh fish, a delicate hand is needed to cook it properly; it should be translucent in the center and warm, but not hot. A restaurant trick to avoid lumps in polenta is to stir it into some cold water to form a slurry. This is then poured slowly, with whisking, into the cooking liquid. Dried mushrooms may be used for the ragout. Reconstitute them in warm water for 30 minutes. Drain and use the soaking liquid in the sauce (3 ounces dry mushrooms = 1 pound fresh).

For the swordfish:

2 tablespoons peanut oil
4 (6–8-ounce) swordfish fillets
2 tablespoons butter
3 sprigs fresh thyme

For the polenta:

7 ounces medium polenta
3 cups chicken stock, simmering
3 tablespoons unsalted butter
2 ounces mascarpone
¼ cup grated Parmesan
½ tablespoon coarse salt
1 tablespoon truffle oil

For the mushroom ragout:

¼ cup canola oil
4 tablespoons unsalted butter
2 tablespoons minced shallots
1 tablespoon minced garlic
5 ounces shiitake mushrooms,
    stems removed, sliced
2 ounces oyster mushrooms, sliced
1 ounce morel mushrooms, cleaned,
    sliced thin
½ cup Chablis

½ cup 10-year-old Taylor Port
¼ cup heavy whipping cream
½ tablespoon coarse salt
½ teaspoon white pepper
1 cup chopped Italian parsley

Heat the peanut oil in a large cast-iron skillet over medium-high heat. Add the fish fillets and sauté 1 minute for color.

Turn the fillets and add the butter and thyme. Place the skillet in a 400°F oven for about 5 minutes, or until the fillets are cooked medium. Be careful not to overcook the fish.

Pour the polenta in a slow, steady stream into the simmering stock, whisking constantly. Cook 40 minutes over low heat, stirring often.

When the polenta is no longer grainy, stir in the mascarpone, Parmesan, salt, and truffle oil. Serve warm.

To prepare the mushroom ragout, heat the canola oil and butter in a large sauté pan over medium heat. Add the shallots and garlic and cook 2 minutes or until the onions are translucent but not browned.

Add the assorted mushrooms and sauté over high heat until the mushrooms release their liquid and begin to brown.

Deglaze the pan with the Chablis and Port. Cook over medium heat and reduce the volume by half. Add the cream and reduce by half again.

Add salt and pepper. Toss in the parsley and stir. Remove from heat immediately.

Place portions of polenta on warm plates. Add a swordfish fillet to each and top with mushroom ragout. Serve immediately.

HUGO'S

MONTROSE
1600 WESTHEIMER ROAD
(713) 524-7744
WWW.HUGOSRESTAURANT.NET
CHEF: HUGO ORTEGA
OWNER: TRACY VAUGHT

The first thing you notice when entering Hugo's is the warm, inviting feel of the interior design. More Spanish than Mexican, the high-back chairs with a hand-tooled look to the fabric welcome you to sit and enjoy Houston's true interior Mexican cuisine. The contrasting cobalt blue water glasses are a striking accent. The waitpersons are knowledgeable and can explain the dishes that may not be immediately familiar to diners.

An example are the *chapulines*, pan-sautéed grasshoppers, a delicacy of Oaxaca, but not so much an American treat. Much less off-putting and delicious are the *sopesitos*, a trio of small rounds of fried cornmeal each topped with a different mixture: lamb with ancho chiles, goat with pasilla chiles, and rabbit with *guajillo adobo*. The suckling pig, *lechón*, is served with the crispy skin and habanero salsa and tortillas, for rolling. Other not-to-miss items include the duck tacos, tacos made with wood-grilled red snapper, and decadent lobster tacos.

One of the best ways to sample a variety of these delicacies is to join in for Sunday brunch, where many menu items are offered on buffet. There is live music from the balcony that is definitely not mariachi, making conversation at the table easy to have. Saturday brunch is menu-driven and allows you to enjoy unique and delicious breakfast items such as poached eggs over sweet corn bread with roasted asparagus, a poblano pepper stuffed with egg, chorizo, and potatoes, or the smoked chicken *chilaquiles*, homemade tortilla chips sautéed with spicy green chiles, tomatillos, and barbecued chicken.

CRABMEAT COCKTAIL

SERVES 4

A restaurant trick to finding all of the bits of shell and cartilage in lump crabmeat is to add it to a metal mixing bowl. As you gently pick through, the shells and such make a "tinkling" sound in the bowl.

8 ounces jumbo lump crabmeat, picked over for cartilage and shell bits
Juice of 1 lime
1 tablespoon olive oil
¼ teaspoon salt
½ cucumber, peeled, thinly sliced
¼ cup cilantro leaves
1 small radish, julienne
2 cups seeded and ¼-inch cubed watermelon
1 red jalapeño, seeded, deveined, julienne
1 large avocado, peeled and cut into ¼-inch cubes

Place the crabmeat in a bowl. Toss with the lime juice, olive oil, and salt, being careful not to break up the crabmeat.

Add the cucumber, cilantro, radish, watermelon, and jalapeño. Toss together gently.

Add the avocado and toss lightly, being careful not to break up the avocado or crabmeat.

Divide the mixture into 4 chilled cocktail or martini glasses and serve immediately.

STREET CARS / MASS TRANSIT

Mule-powered streetcars were Houston's first attempt at mass transit. The very first cars began operation in 1868, but it wasn't until 1874 that the Houston City Street Railway would begin operation and become a traceable descendant of today's METRO system. The Houston Heights line opened in 1892, first as a separate company, then was absorbed into the modernized Houston Electric Street Railway.

By 1914 competition for the commuter came in the form of jitneys, cars for hire running specific routes across the city. For almost a decade jitneys caused havoc with the profitability of the streetcar. Houston eventually outlawed them, and buses replaced them in 1924. One interesting streetcar that became popular at the time, with cities both large and small, was the "Birney One Man Streetcar," a small, single-truck trolley that could be operated by one person safely and economically. The last streetcars were purchased in 1927, and the last run of an electric streetcar was in June 1940. Almost nothing remains of the streetcar system. No rails remain embedded in any street, and no buildings associated with the system are left standing. Much of the loss is due to the beginning of World War II when scrap drives claimed the metal rails and car parts to recycle them for the war effort.

Beef & Pork Meatballs in Spicy Broth with Vegetables

SERVES 8

One way to instantly improve the taste of home-cooked foods is to grind your own meat. In addition to a remarkable flavor, freshly ground meat from bulk cuts are not contaminated with *E. coli* (which comes from unsanitary handling of ground meat) and can be cooked rare if desired.

½ teaspoon whole cumin seeds

4 whole black peppercorns

1 small bay leaf

1 whole clove

1 pound pork shoulder, cut into ½-inch cubes

8 ounces ground beef

1 egg

2 sprigs mint, finely chopped

1½ tablespoons cooked rice, puréed

1 corn tortilla, soaked, puréed

2 Roma tomatoes, roasted, peeled and seeded, chopped

6 canned chipotle peppers with sauce, seeded

½ teaspoon chicken base

½ tablespoon lard

1 tablespoon minced white onion

1 garlic clove, minced

4 cups water

1 small calabacita squash, washed, cut into ½-inch cubes

1 small carrot, peeled, cut into ½-inch cubes

1 Yukon Gold potato, peeled, cut into ½-inch cubes

1 sprig cilantro, finely chopped

2 mint leaves, finely chopped (chop just before using)

Salt and pepper

Combine the cumin seeds, black peppercorns, bay leaf, and clove in a spice grinder or blender and grind to a fine powder.

Grind the pork shoulder through the fine plate of a meat grinder. Mix thoroughly with the ground beef and spice mixture. Add the eggs, mint, rice, and tortilla and mix to thoroughly combine.

Roll 1 tablespoon portions of meat mixture into small meatballs. Reserve.

Add half of the chopped tomatoes, the chipotle peppers with their sauce, and chicken base to a blender and purée until smooth. Transfer to a bowl with the remaining chopped tomatoes.

Place the lard in a 3-quart saucepan over medium heat and allow it to almost reach its smoking point. Lower the heat and add the onion and garlic. Cook until the onion is translucent, about 3 minutes.

Add the tomato mixture and sauté 2 minutes. Add the water and bring it to a boil. When boiling, add the tiny meatballs. Lower the heat and allow them to simmer for 10 minutes.

Add the squash, carrot, and potato and cook until done, about 10 minutes. Add the chopped cilantro and mint and cook 2 more minutes. Adjust seasoning with salt and pepper.

Huynh

EaDo (East of Downtown)
912 St. Emanuel Street
(713) 224-8964
www.huynhrestauranthouston.com
Chef/Owners: Van Bui and Anny Dang

This is not your typical Vietnamese pho restaurant, which are becoming so common across America. Nestled in a strip center in the up-and-coming EaDo district, Huynh, which opened in 2008, offers up authentic dishes right from the streets and alleyways of Vietnam. Uplifted in a tastefully designed space, it has just the right touch of modern urban mixed with restrained Asian decor.

This is Van Bui's second foray into the restaurant business, after working hard and eventually purchasing the original Pho Huynh in 1998, eight years after arriving in America with no money and little English. Her flavors are delicate yet pronounced, with ingredients carefully sought out to replicate those found in the owners' homeland. Something as simple as Vietnamese iced coffee is crafted with three different coffee beans imported from Vietnam. The perfect sweetened condensed milk is not exported to the United States and frustrates Anny, Van's daughter, to no end. This passionate caring for authenticity makes even the simplest dishes rise to subtle perfection. Shredded duck meat with fresh herbs and ginger dipping sauce is exquisite, and the grilled short ribs will haunt you to return.

FIRM TOFU WITH TOMATO

SERVES 2

Tofu means "curdled bean" and is made from curdling soy milk with certain salts or enzymes. The resulting solids (curds) are added directly to the packaging container for soft or silken tofu, or are pressed into blocks to remove excess moisture before packaging when making firm tofu.

2 tablespoons peanut oil

1-inch piece leek, white part only,
   cut into matchsticks

1 garlic clove, minced

8 ounces firm or extra-firm tofu,
   cut into ¼-inch cubes

1 medium heirloom tomato,
   seeded and chopped

½ teaspoon minced fresh hot red chile

½ tablespoon sugar

1 tablespoon soy sauce

Black pepper

Heat the oil in a nonstick skillet over medium-high heat. Add the leek and garlic and sauté until fragrant. Be careful not to burn the garlic.

Add the tofu and sauté lightly. Add the chopped tomato and cook it until tomato starts to break down, about 3 minutes.

Reduce the heat to low and add the chile. Stir in the sugar and soy sauce. Cook 1 minute. Adjust seasoning with soy sauce and sugar. Add black pepper to taste. Serve immediately.

Beef Croustades

SERVES 4

A croustade is a French term for crust and can refer to a pie crust, puff pastry round, or a bread slice that has been toasted for a topping.

2 garlic cloves, peeled and crushed

4 ounces (½ cup) butter

24 (¼-inch) slices baguette or other round bread

1 egg yolk

1 tablespoon Dijon mustard

1 cup canola oil

3 fluid ounces rice wine vinegar

Pinch dried dill

Pinch fresh parsley

1 garlic clove, minced

Pinch dried thyme

1 tablespoon Worcestershire sauce

3 fluid ounces olive oil

1 teaspoon seasoned salt

3 tablespoons Creole mustard

12 ounces roasted beef tenderloin,
    cut into 24 thin slices

Add the crushed garlic to the butter in a microwave-proof cup or dish. Microwave on high to melt the butter, about 1 minute. Allow to stand 5 minutes

Brush each bread slice with garlic butter and place the bread slices on a baking sheet. Toast the bread in a 400°F oven until golden, about 5 minutes.

Whisk the egg yolk with the Dijon mustard. Slowly whisk in the canola oil, alternating with the rice wine vinegar.

Add the dill, fresh parsley, garlic, thyme, and Worcestershire sauce. Stir to incorporate.

Whisk in the olive oil gradually. Stir in the seasoned salt and Creole mustard. Refrigerate until needed.

To serve, place 6 toasts on a plate. Top each toast with a slice of beef tenderloin and add some mustard sauce to each, using a squeeze bottle to form stripes or a Z pattern.

SPARKLE'S CHILL SPOT
1515 Dowling Street

One of Houston's gems, this unassuming, bright-blue restaurant is run by Sparkle Chantale Steels. This gal knows how to eliminate hunger. Order a single-patty burger and you will understand. Hand-formed from quality ground beef, the cooked burger looks like a family-size meat loaf resting in an oversized bun and weighed in at close to 16 ounces before cooking. With the requisite lettuce, tomato, onions, and pickles, this is easily a meal for two hungry persons. At $4 this sandwich is the bargain of all food bargains. Add cheese for no additional cost. Add a second patty (why on earth would you?) for two bucks more.

It takes a while to cook a burger this big, so you may want to call in and give Sparkle at least fifteen minutes to prepare it. There are two picnic tables under a lonely oak tree, but most customers drive up and go with their order. Non-burger items include breakfast sandwiches (try the pork chop and egg) and Cajun platters, called 'n'waffles—chicken, pork chop, fish, fried or grilled chicken tenders or breast, ground beef, or shrimp. Try their seafood platters, salads, or stuffed baked potato for a change of pace.

PAT AND JOE'S BELLAIRE BROILER BURGER
5216 Bellaire Boulevard

This classic burger joint has been serving up great flame-broiled hamburgers since 1957, when it was called Briton's Broiler Burger. Pat and Joe purchased it in 1972, and it is still family run by their son. Very little has changed since 1957, other than the prices, and the only difference in the burgers is that they now offer a wheat bun. Regular burgers come classically dressed with lettuce, tomatoes, onion, pickles, and your choice of mustard, mayo, or barbecue sauce. Traditional add-ons include cheese, bacon, mushrooms, or jalapeños.

If you can't make up your mind between a burger and a hot dog, try the combination special of a hamburger patty and two grilled franks on a bun, topped with chili, cheese, and onion. Their Chili Delight is a "casserole" open-face double burger topped with chili, grated cheese, and onions for those of you torn between a burger and chili. They offer larger meat patties with their extra-large burger, and the Bellaire Special is perfect for those craving a satisfying meal on a bun: two four-ounce patties, cheese, grilled bacon, and all of the vegetables. Non-burger menu items include chicken tenders with gravy or barbecue sauce, a marinated chicken breast sandwich, a double-decker with ham and bacon, grilled cheese, or a chef's salad. The onion rings are hand-dipped and are noteworthy.

LANKFORD'S CAFE
88 Dennis Street

Lankford's Cafe is still referred to as the Grocery and Market, although it was in the 1990s that the spot transitioned to an exclusively dining venue. Opened in 1938 as a neighborhood grocery and in this location since 1939, Lankford's served its first deli sandwich in the early 1970s. By 1980 hamburgers were added to the menu, and the first lunch special, the enchilada dinner, was introduced. This plate is still offered every Wednesday exactly as originally made. Chicken-fried steak is on the Thursday lunch special, and Friday is Super Taco Dinner. Monday and Tuesday are pot luck, listed as Chef's Choice.

But the burgers are the star here, and the eight-ounce patty comes dressed with mayo, mustard, lettuce, and tomato as standard. The Firehouse burger adds habanero sauce and the not-to-be-missed Soldier burger adds a fried egg. For the cholesterol conscious, avoid the fabulous Grim Burger, which sports mac and cheese, bacon, and a fried egg. Sides include classic tater tots and Tex Mex, which is a combination of strips of jalapeños and onions golden batter fried. Respectable non-burger selections include a BLT, tuna melt, chicken sliders, grilled cheese, or a club sandwich. For a light meal, the chef's salad or tossed green salad comes with house-made dressings and fresh vegetables.

BECK'S PRIME
2902 Kirby Drive

For more than twenty-five years, Beck's Prime has been serving up the ultimate in fast food. Kirby Drive is the original location, and there are now two more: one downtown on Travis and the other on the Memorial Loop. Their burgers are some of the best to be found in Houston, or anywhere for that matter. The meat is ground fresh daily in-store, hand-formed, and cooked over mesquite coals. The buns are noteworthy, similar to brioche or challah. Everything is prepared from scratch, which makes the fries a must to order, especially the sweet potato fries, which are outstanding. Standard burger fixings include lettuce, tomato, pickle, and mustard. Prime sauce, a homemade, flavored

mayo spread, can be added to make a B.P. burger. Other choices are hickory sauce, bacon, chili, blue cheese, Swiss, and cheddar.

A favorite is the Bill's Burger with sautéed onions, sliced cheddar, bacon, jalapeños, prime sauce, and lettuce. The TKO features chili and hickory sauce, and the California adds guacamole and Swiss. For the hot dog aficionado, Boars' Head makes a custom quarter-pound frank to Beck's exacting specifications; you can order it chili-cheese style, with kraut and mustard, or "old-fashioned" with mustard, pickle, and onion. Rounding out the menu is a variety of mesquite-grilled chicken, ahi tuna, rib eye, and tenderloin sand-wiches, a BLT, and a veggie burger.

HUBCAP GRILL
1111 Prairie Street

It doesn't matter whose list you check for best burgers in Houston, whether it be a newspaper article or one of the Internet foodie sites, Hubcap Grill is always mentioned in the top five. It's a tiny sliver of a restaurant next to the Alden Hotel in Downtown, with a modest counter and a couple of tables inside, and more seating outside on the sidewalk and under umbrellas on the side of the building.

Owner Ricky Craig has recently opened a second location in the Heights and he is now able to serve more of his hand-crafted burgers, many of which are creatively fashioned like no other hamburger you've eaten. The muffalletta burger is topped with house-made olive mix dressing, Swiss, and special mayo sauce. A Greek burger has melted feta, slices of kalamata olives, and green peppers, while the Sticky Burger is topped with peanut butter, bacon, and cheese. The Triple Heart Clogger combines a fresh one-third-pound, hand-formed burger patty with a grilled hot dog, bacon, and cheese, and it can be converted into a Quadruple by adding chili. The Philly Cheese Steak burger has sliced rib eye and sautéed onions, green peppers, and melting cheese topping their famous patty.

If you'd prefer a chicken sandwich, they are offered in most of the styles of their beef burgers. The buns are homemade as are their fries. Rather than soda fountain soft drinks, which can be variable in quality, the owners believe the best sodas come from bottles.

BERNIE'S BURGER BUS
call (281) 386-2447 or visit berniesburgerbus.com for location and schedule

One of the hottest new trends in dining out is the food trailer and food truck. Food trailers are semi-permanent and are usually located in clusters (called pods in Portland, Oregon), offering a variety of foods, beverages, and desserts, much like a food court at the mall, but different in that the food is often unique and of very high quality. Food trucks are mobile and usually rely on electronic social media such as Facebook and Twitter to alert the public of their locations. Local regulations define how mobile these facilities must be. Bernie's Burger Bus is painted as a school bus, so it is easy to identify when looking for its spot. Lately the Bus has been regularly at the same parking lot on certain days of the week.

Bernie's menu goes with the school theme and names the burgers accordingly. The Principal is the basic burger with lettuce, onions, pickles, mayo, mustard, and ketchup. A signature topping is their slow-roasted garlic tomatoes. Add-ons include cheddar, applewood-smoked bacon, and Bernie's Caramelized Tipsy Onions. The Substitute tops their fresh patty, nestled in a fresh, baked-daily bun, with blue cheese, bacon, Burgundy sautéed mushrooms, and caramelized onions. The luscious Homeroom tops a cheddar-, bacon-, caramelized-onion burger with chipotle aioli and a fried egg, but the hunger-busting, cholesterol-elevating jewel of this menu is the Detention. Two patties are nestled between two bacon grilled cheese sandwiches that substitute for a bun. Texas cheddar adds even more cheese to this heart attack on a plate that is finished with caramelized onions and all the fixings.

At the opposite end of this scale are the Kindergartners and Pre-Schoolers, mini-sliders with assorted toppings. There are burger specials (Field Trip), a grilled cheese sandwich on local sourdough bread (Recess), and Extra Curricular Activities—fries with homemade ketchup; fries seasoned with Parmesan, green onion, and truffle oil; blue cheese fries with bacon and green onions; and sweet potato fries served with chipotle aioli. The bus is small and everything is cooked to order, so come early or late or be prepared to wait for your order.

IBIZA FOOD AND WINE BAR

MIDTOWN
2450 LOUISIANA STREET
(713) 524-0004
WWW.IBIZAFOODANDWINEBAR.COM
CHEF/OWNER: CHARLES CLARK

A confluence of styles swirls together on the menu of this chic and modern restaurant. Bent oak chairs and starched white tablecloths welcome you to watch the activity of the open kitchen busily constructing dishes inspired from Spain, of Creole origin, and modern American fare. Chef/Owner Charles Clark is hands-on, ensuring every dish meets his exacting specifications. The wine pricing is especially attractive, bordering on what you would expect to pay retail, with little additional mark-up.

In addition to stressing only the finest ingredients, both local and imported, the food and menu are perceived a good value. When Charles can get it (it is listed "as available" on the menu), *burrata* is featured in salads and on pizzas, but it is imported from Italy and is not always on hand. Rich, buttery, and soft, burrata is made by encasing cream and mozzarella in a cover of mozzarella cheese. It shows its best characteristics at Ibiza as a salad when paired with arugula, basil, ripe tomatoes, and olive oil. Roasted peppercorn powder finishes this simple yet elegant starter.

The lobster risotto may be the best rice dish ever. The lobster is carefully prepared so as not to be overcooked. It's paired with a fresh pea broth and some freshly shucked corn kernels. Texturally it is superb. The lobster is soft and yielding while the rice is chewy to the tooth and the corn pops when bitten. Pan-seared Koiak island halibut is perfectly cooked, and the richness of the flesh is balanced with a vinaigrette of sesame and mango.

Spanish-influenced dishes abound, such as plancha-grilled octopus with Spanish chorizo, and pickled white anchovies (*bocarones*) dressed simply with quality olive oil and fresh parsley. Spanish piquillo peppers stuffed with herbed cheese, Basque green pepper and crab bisque, roasted beets with Spanish goat cheese, and gazpacho in the style of southern Spain all draw upon Iberian influences. Don't miss the Creole-inspired dishes, especially the crab cake with smoked jalapeño rouille or the pan-fried oysters with Tasso cream. If you can fit dessert in, the carrot cake done as a multilayered torte is exceptional and is served with house-made blood orange sorbet and garnished with candied carrot slivers.

Rigatoncini with Pesto, Fregola, Roasted Chicken & Portobellos

SERVES 6

Fregola is a Sardinian specialty pasta similar to Israeli couscous, rolled into small balls and toasted in ovens prior to cooking.

1 (2-pound) chicken

2 teaspoons sea salt

2 teaspoons fresh ground black pepper

¼ cup roasted garlic

2 tablespoons extra-virgin olive oil

3 garlic cloves, peeled

2 cups lightly packed fresh basil leaves

3 tablespoons pine nuts

¾ cup extra-virgin olive oil

1 teaspoon coarse salt

3 portobello mushrooms, cleaned,
    dark gills scooped out with a spoon

Olive oil

Salt and pepper

½ cup orzo pasta, precooked and set aside warm
    (or fregola from Sardinia, if available)

1 pound rigatoncini pasta (or other small
    hollow pasta), precooked and set aside warm

½ cup roasted corn kernels

4 piquillo peppers, drained from the jar and diced

¼ cup thinly shaved Parmigiana Reggiano

3 tablespoons grated pecorino Romano

Season the chicken with salt, pepper, garlic, and 2 tablespoons olive oil. Roast in a 375°F oven for 1 hour or until chicken registers 165°F in a thigh. Allow to cool.

Add the garlic cloves, basil, pine nuts, ¾ cup olive oil, and salt to food processor and purée until the pesto is smooth. Reserve.

Brush the mushrooms with olive oil, salt, and pepper.

Using a large sauté pan over high heat, sear the mushrooms on both sides briefly. Transfer to 400°F oven and roast for 10 minutes. Set aside to cool.

Slice the cooled mushrooms very thin.

Pull the meat from chicken and shred, using some of the crisp, golden skin.

In a large mixing bowl add both warm pastas and toss with the pesto. Add the roasted corn and diced peppers. Toss in the sliced mushrooms and pulled chicken. Gently fold in the two cheeses.

Serve warm or at room temperature.

Piquillo Peppers Stuffed with Local Goat Cheese & Porcini

SERVES 6

Piquillo peppers are from northern Spain and are roasted over embers, seeded by hand, and packaged, usually in jars, ready to be stuffed. They are quite popular as tapas, stuffed with meats, seafood, and/or cheeses.

1 pound goat cheese, at room temperature

2 tablespoons porcini powder

18 Spanish piquillo peppers, drained from a can or jar

1 cup chopped tomatoes

1 tablespoon roasted garlic

1 tablespoon minced basil

1 tablespoon minced red onion

2 tablespoons olive oil

10 ounces cleaned spinach

Salt and pepper

Preheat the oven to 350°F. Using an electric mixer with the whip attachment, place the goat cheese in a mixing bowl. Add the porcini powder and mix until uniform.

Using a pastry bag (or a ziplock bag with a bottom corner cut off), loosely pipe the cheese mixture into the peppers. Do not allow the cheese to overflow.

Place the stuffed peppers on a nonstick (or parchment-lined) cookie sheet and bake for 5 to 7 minutes in the preheated oven.

In a sauté pan, add the tomatoes, garlic, basil, onion, and 1 tablespoon of the olive oil and bring to a simmer.

Mix in the spinach and the remaining olive oil, cooking over medium heat until the spinach is slightly wilted, about 30 seconds. Season the mixture with salt and pepper.

Place a portion of spinach mixture on each plate and top with 3 stuffed peppers. Serve immediately.

INDIKA

MONTROSE
516 WESTHEIMER ROAD
(713) 524-2170
WWW.INDIKAUSA.COM
OWNERS: ANITA AND RAVI JAISINGHANI

Montrose is a neighborhood known for its eclectic style and restaurants of myriad ethnic cuisines. Indika is a perfect example. Indika serves up exceptional Indian food in an uncluttered, modern space that avoids the trappings of being overly decorated. Lofty ceilings and a cool color palette make for a relaxed dining experience. Chef/Owner Anita Jaisinghani seeks to obtain the freshest ingredients and combines them with a strong, yet sensible amount of spice.

Spice-crusted sea bass is such a dish. The sweetness of the fillet comes only from careful selection of a fishmonger's offerings. The coconut milk and saffron broth is bright but does not overpower the delicate nature of the sea bass, and the grapefruit lime pickle on top adds a final note of sparkle. The corn and mint *chaat* salad is light and refreshing; the braised lamb leg in cashew cardamom curry is intense.

When you think you have figured out the style of the food, bread pudding with Valrhona chocolate and delicate, moist, buttery brioche laced with soft custard comes to the table, highlighting Chef Anita's desire to master European baking in her spare time, of which she has little since opening Pondicheri, an all-day restaurant serving Indian street food. Indika offers cooking classes for cooks of all skill levels and is a great way to explore authentic Indian food preparation.

SEAFOOD MULLIGATAWNY SOUP

SERVES 6

This soup is of British-Indian origin during colonial times. In Tamil *milagu* means pepper and *thani* translates as water, although this delicious soup can be so much more than pepper water. It is usually curry based. The medicinal-tasting herb curry leaf (no relationship to curry powder) can be obtained from most Indian markets.

½ cup yellow split lentils

2 cups chopped cauliflower florets

1 large carrot, peeled, cut into thick slices

2-inch piece ginger, unpeeled, chopped

2 sprigs curry leaf

2 Serrano peppers, minced

1 cup coconut milk

6 cups chicken stock

2 teaspoons salt

12 mussels

12 large shrimp

12 large scallops

2 tablespoons corn oil

1 teaspoon mustard seed

Juice of 1 lemon

½ teaspoon garam masala

2 tablespoons chopped cilantro

Rinse the lentils in warm water and then soak them for 1 to 2 hours.

Add the soaked lentils to a large saucepan or pot along with the cauliflower, carrot, ginger, curry leaf, peppers, coconut milk, and 4 cups of chicken stock. Cook over medium-low heat 45 minutes to 1 hour, until vegetables are soft and lentils tender.

When cooked, add the soup to a blender or processor (in portions if needed) and purée until smooth. Return the purée to the pot and add the remaining chicken stock. Adjust seasoning with salt.

Add the seafood and bring to a boil. Lower the heat and simmer for 3 to 4 minutes and then remove from the heat.

Heat the corn oil in a small skillet over low heat. Add the mustard seed and cook until they pop. Add this to the soup along with the lemon juice, garam masala, and cilantro. Serve immediately.

KATA ROBATA

RIVER OAKS
3600 KIRBY LANE
(713) 526-8858
WWW.KATAROBATA.COM
CHEF: MANABU HORIUCHI
OWNER: THE AZUMA GROUP

This is the hot place in town. Located in upscale River Oaks, Kata is on the cutting edge of sushi meets molecular gastronomy. Chef Manabu Horiuchi, a top chef with Michelin star credentials from Japan, applied his Japanese sensibilities to Seth Seigel-Gardner's laboratory-driven twenty-first-century techniques for manipulating food (in a good way).

The food is passion driven, and the passion is derived from every employee, from dishwasher to head chef, each one willing to contribute whatever they can to the success of the food experience. The result is seared Washington state Quillaute salmon with foamed ponzu sauce and smoked tomato powder, foie gras terrine topped with *unagi* (marinated eel), and bluefin tuna and snapper sashimi with uni powder. The uni powder is made by freezing sea urchin roe in liquid nitrogen and blending it into a powder while rock solid, then freezing until needed. As it thaws, essence of urchin infuses whatever it has been dusted on. There's lobster macaroni and cheese and pork belly don made from Berkshire pork, a farm-fresh egg, Japanese mushrooms, and pickles. In a sushi assortment a surprise awaits at the end with lightly blanched *hamachi* filled with a gently poached quail egg.

General Manager Josh Martinez is the mastermind behind the infusion drinks that are over-the-top creative. He uses *sous vide* techniques—vacuum sealing and slow, low-temperature cooking—to infuse whiskeys and other alcohol with fresh herbs and savory notes. These preparations are then barrel-aged for months in the attic above the restaurant. In one recipe, Josh uses the fat from the foie gras terrine and mixes it with whiskey. He then vacuum seals it and cooks it over low heat. To remove the fat he uses liquid nitrogen and carefully filters any remnants of congealed duck fat, forming a clear infusion ready for barrel aging.

"Kakuni" Braised Pork Belly

SERVES 4

Once considered a cheap, leftover cut of meat, pork belly has become popular with today's creative chefs (and is no longer cheap). It is the meat from which bacon is made and when slowly cooked becomes buttery, rich, and fork-tender.

1 pound pork belly

8 cups water

1 (2-inch) piece ginger, sliced

1 bunch green onions, sliced

3 cups sake

3 cups dashi

1 cup Coca-Cola

¾ cup soy sauce

⅓ cup sugar

2 tablespoons brown sugar

1 (2-inch) piece ginger

6 egg yolks

1 teaspoon lemon juice

1 tablespoon Dijon mustard

1 cup micro greens

Cut pork belly into 2½-inch cubes. Sear the cubes in a hot skillet until golden brown.

Place the browned pork belly in the water in a large saucepan. Add the ginger and green onion and simmer over low heat for 4 hours.

Carefully drain the pork and reserve. Toss out the ginger, green onions, and simmering liquid.

Add the sake, dashi, Coca-Cola, soy sauce, both sugars, and the ginger to a large, nonreactive saucepan. Add the pork cubes and simmer over low heat about 5 hours. Be careful not to break up the pork cubes when handling or transferring them. Add water as necessary.

Allow to cool. Carefully transfer the pork to a container and refrigerate until needed. Before serving, warm the pork in a 325°F oven for 15 minutes on a parchment-lined sheet pan.

Strain and reduce the poaching sauce over medium heat until thick and syrupy. Reserve.

Whisk to make a foam of the egg yolks, lemon juice, and mustard.

To serve, place portions of micro greens on small plates. Add the braised pork belly and top each piece with mustard foam. Serve immediately.

Scallop & Foie Gras Sushi

SERVES 2

At first glance this seems an odd combination. Texturally it works quite well, and the inherent sweetness of scallops complements the foie gras, as it is often served with a sweet component.

For the eel sauce (makes 2 cups):

8 cups water

2 cups sake

2½ cups sugar

1⅔ cups soy sauce

For the scallops and foie gras:

2 large (size U10) sashimi-grade scallops, each sliced horizontally into 3 pieces

2 (1½-ounce) portions foie gras, veins removed

Flour for dusting

Salt

2 fluid ounces eel sauce (see recipe steps)

½ cup cooked sushi rice

2 strips nori, cut into 3-inch x ½-inch strips

Make the eel sauce by adding the water, sake, 1¾ cups sugar, and 1 cup soy sauce to a nonreactive saucepan. Cook over medium-low heat to reduce volume by half.

Add the remaining sugar and soy sauce and simmer over low heat 2 hours until sauce is thick and sticky.

Using a torch, brown one side of each scallop slice. Reserve.

Dust the foie gras with flour and salt. Sear in a very hot skillet 1 minute on each side.

Brush each piece of *foie gras* with eel sauce.

Add sushi rice to 2 small plates. Lay slices of scallop across the rice. Top with glazed *foie gras*. Wrap each with a band of nori and serve immediately.

LATIN BITES CAFE

GALLERIA
5709 WOODWAY DRIVE
(713) 229-8369
WWW.LATINBITESCAFE.COM
CHEF/OWNERS: ROBERTO CASTRE AND CARLOS RAMOS

Originally located in a very small space in the Old Art's Warehouse District north of downtown, Latin Bites Cafe has moved into a much roomier space, tripling the seating capacity. This allows more diners access to one of the best ethnic restaurants in the city, hosted by owner and partner Carlos Ramos. Peruvian cuisine is not very well known to most, but the flavors are.

Expect bright and fully seasoned sauces, the heat of chiles (not too spicy), and the tang of citrus. Ceviches and *sashimi tiraditos* start with the freshest of white-fleshed fish, which are marinated in lime juice and chile. The marinade is called *leche de tigres* (tiger's milk) and comes in three varieties, based on the chile used. These chiles are Peruvian and may not be familiar to most diners: *aji amarillo*, *limo*, and *rocoto*. The limo is quite spicy and is related to the habanero, as is the rocoto, also known as the manzano chile. The most commonly used chile in Peruvian cuisine is the *aji amarillo*, a slender chile of medium spiciness that practically defines Peruvian cuisine. Empanadas are found across South America, and the Latin Bites version is meaty and rich with tender and flaky pastry.

Don't miss the assorted fried fish and seafood appetizer, *Jalea de Peascados & Mariscos*, with perfectly battered and fried fish fillets, octopus, squid, and shrimp served with a spicy *rocoto* mayonnaise and salsa *criolla*. Meat entrees include slow-cooked lamb stew served with a traditional pancake made from rice and beans (*tacu tacu*), grilled rib eye with chimichurri sauce, and a twenty-four-hour marinated chicken served with a creamy cilantro sauce.

There is an interesting Chinese influence to Peruvian cooking, and the fried rice with chicken, pork, and beef is a perfect example of this hybrid cuisine. Paella done Peruvian style is a spectacular rendition. Chef and owner Roberto Castre shines when it comes to fish and seafood, and the sautéed fish fillet with a cream sauce of panca peppers and pisco, topped with clams, mussels, squid, and octopus, is a star of the menu. Garnishing many of the dishes are fried, dried corn kernels and giant fresh Peruvian corn kernels, which are also served as snacks with drinks. For a unique, refreshing beverage, order the *chicha morada*, a fruit punch made from purple corn, apples, and cinnamon.

Pescado a Lo Macho

SERVES 2

A defining ingredient in Peruvian cuisine is the yellow chile, *aji amarillo*. Despite its name, the chile is bright orange when ripe. *Aji rocoto* is another common chile, much hotter than the *amarillo*, and can stand much colder temperatures than other chiles, allowing them to flourish in the high Andes.

¼ cup vegetable oil

¾ cup finely diced white onion

4 garlic cloves, finely minced

6 medium shrimp, peeled, shells used for the sauce

1 tomato, peeled, seeded, and finely chopped

1 tablespoon aji amarillo molido (crushed yellow Peruvian chile)

1 tablespoon of ají panca molido (crushed panca chile)

½ cup white wine

2 tablespoons Peruvian pisco

¼ cup cream

Salt and pepper

6 clams, scrubbed

4 mussels, scrubbed, beards removed

6 ounces squid tubes, cut into rings

6 ounces cooked octopus, cut into ½-inch slices

1 teaspoon ground cumin (comino)

2 fish fillets, 6 ounces each, such as cod, snapper, or sea bass

Oil to sauté

2 cups cooked white rice

2 small Yukon Gold potatoes, peeled, boiled, halved, and seared in butter

2 small limes, quartered

Fresh cilantro for garnish

Heat the oil in large skillet over medium heat. Add the onion, garlic, and the shrimp shells. Sauté 2 minutes.

Add the tomatoes and crushed chiles and sauté 2 minutes. Add the wine and pisco and raise the heat to a boil.

Add the cream and lower the heat to a simmer. Cook until the sauce coats the back of a spoon. Season with salt and pepper and allow the sauce to cool slightly off heat. Strain and reserve the sauce.

In a hot skillet add the clams and cook 1 minute, shaking the pan. Add the mussels and repeat. Add the shrimp and sauté 2 minutes.

Add the squid and the octopus, stirring briefly. Add the sauce and simmer 1 minute. Add the cumin and adjust seasoning with salt and pepper.

In a small skillet sauté the fillets in some oil to brown both sides. Place the pan in a 400°F oven for 5 minutes, or until the fish is flaking and just cooked through.

Place each fillet on a plate and distribute the seafood evenly. Cover with sauce. Add a timbale of rice and a cooked potato to each plate. Garnish with lime slices and cilantro.

PERUVIAN SASHIMI WITH THREE SAUCES

TIRADITO TRES SABORES

SERVES 2

There is a strong connection between Peru and Japan, both historically and from a culinary viewpoint. Peru was the first Latin American country to establish diplomatic relations with Japan, allowing Japanese immigration in 1899. This dish points out the connection quite well.

2 garlic cloves, crushed

1 stalk celery, chopped

1 (2-inch) piece ginger, peeled and cut into ½-inch slices

½ cup sliced leeks, white part only

½ cup diced white onion

1 cup whole milk

3 ounces sashimi-grade yellowtail fillet (hamachi) or other fresh fillet, minced

¼ cup lime juice

1 cup peanut oil

2 tablespoons white vinegar

Salt and pepper

1 tablespoon ají amarillo chile paste

1 tablespoon aji rocoto chile paste

1 small sweet potato, peeled and cut into 1-inch cubes

1 cup orange juice

1½ cups sugar

15 choclo (giant Peruvian) corn kernels (or other corn variety if necessary)

6 ounces sashimi-grade yellowtail fillet (hamachi), thinly sliced as for sashimi

Chopped green onion

Olive oil

Place the garlic, celery, ginger, leek, and white onion with the milk and enough water to cover in a saucepan and cook over low heat, simmering 2 minutes. Strain, reserving the liquid. Allow the poaching liquid to cool to room temperature.

Mix 3 ounces of minced fish with the lime juice, oil, vinegar, and poaching liquid. Season with salt and pepper. Refrigerate the sauce 2 hours.

Divide the sauce into 3 equal parts. Mix 1 part with ají amarillo chile paste, 1 part with rocoto chile paste, and leave the last part plain. Refrigerate until needed.

Simmer the diced sweet potato with the orange juice and 1 cup sugar until tender, about 8 minutes. Allow to cool.

Simmer the corn kernels in 1 cup water with ½ cup sugar. Allow to cool.

Arrange slices of yellowtail on plates. Sprinkle with salt and pepper. Lay the 3 sauces, in bands, across the fish slices. Top with green onion and a drizzle of olive oil. Add potato and corn on the side. Serve immediately.

Line and Lariat

Downtown
Hotel ICON, 220 Main Street
(832) 667-4470
www.hotelicon.com/dining-2
Chef: David Luna
Owner: Marriot Hotel Group

Nestled in the boutique hotel ICON, a refurbished 100-year-old bank building in downtown Houston, lies Line and Lariat, an open and eclectically designed restaurant speaking new Texas cuisine. The hotel has recently been purchased by Magic Johnson of basketball fame, and an infusion of money and style certainly follows. The restaurant has seen a change in name and direction, from the more broadly American cuisine of VOICE to the regional cuisine approach of Line and Lariat.

Chef Luna is particular about his produce and seeks locally grown whenever possible. His delicate touch allows the freshness to shine through, and his preparations are never fussy or contrived. One of the hardest things to do as a chef is to make things simple. It requires a true understanding of flavor and how ingredients interact. Chef Luna has this understanding.

Starters on the menu that reflect this include sweet corn cakes with chipotle shrimp and cornmeal-crusted Gulf fried oysters with ancho honey. As an entree, the Gulf shrimp are paired with crawfish grits, a simple, yet elegant, local combination. Texas quail with a Shiner Bock molasses glaze is a clever pairing, and there's plenty of beef to satisfy the hearty Texan diner, including a skirt steak with a three-cheese enchilada side. The simply prepared roast chicken is juicy and moist, as is the pork tenderloin.

Marinated Pork Tenderloin with Pan-Roasted Mushrooms

SERVES 4

Other mushrooms would work well in this dish, especially shiitake. Remove the tough stems with scissors before using. Portobello mushrooms are crimini mushrooms that have been allowed to grow large. If using portobellos, remove the dark gills with a spoon to prevent them from imparting a murky color to the dish.

For the pork:

1 cup pure olive oil
¼ cup soy sauce
1 teaspoon minced garlic
½ teaspoon fresh ground black pepper
1 teaspoon chopped fresh thyme leaves
1 teaspoon brown sugar
4 (6-ounce) portions pork tenderloin, trimmed
Peanut oil

For the mushrooms:

¼ cup pure olive oil
4 cups crimini mushrooms, cleaned,
    sliced ⅛ inch thick
2 tablespoons unsalted butter
Fresh chopped thyme
Salt and pepper

Mix the olive oil, soy sauce, garlic, pepper, thyme, and brown sugar together.

Place the pork tenderloin portions in a resealable plastic bag and add the marinade. Refrigerate at least 4 hours or overnight.

Heat some peanut oil in a heavy skillet. Pat the tenderloins dry and brown them in the oil on all sides until golden.

Place the skillet in a 400°F oven for 8 to 10 minutes or until tenderloins are cooked medium.

Heat a large skillet with the oil over medium heat. Toss in the mushrooms and sauté until the mushrooms soften and release their moisture, but do not brown.

Add the butter and thyme and cook until the mushrooms have released their liquid and are soft.

Continue to cook until the edges brown and the liquid is almost gone. Adjust seasoning with salt and pepper. Serve immediately.

Slice each portion on the diagonal and arrange the slices on warm plates. Serve with pan-roasted mushrooms.

LEMON GARLIC CHICKEN WITH BUTTERNUT SQUASH

SERVES 4

Brining is the key to the tenderness and juiciness of this dish's roasted chicken breast, which can often be dry, even when carefully cooked. Brining causes cells to retain water after absorbing salt. The amount of time that meat is left in a salt solution should be carefully monitored, as too much time gives a cured texture and salty flavor to the meat.

For the chicken:

4 (12-ounce) bone-in chicken breasts
    with wing attached
2 cups coarse salt dissolved in
    2 quarts cold water
Pure olive oil
4 garlic cloves, sliced
2 tablespoons butter
8 lemon slices, ⅛ inch thick
¼ cup chicken stock
2 tablespoons lemon juice

For the butternut squash:

1 butternut squash, peeled, quartered,
    seeded
¼ cup extra-virgin olive oil
Salt and pepper
2 tablespoons orange juice
2 tablespoons butter

Brine the chicken by soaking in salt solution 4 hours. Drain and pat dry.

Sauté the chicken breasts in a large skillet over medium-high heat with olive oil to brown and crisp the skin.

Turn the chicken breasts and add the garlic and butter. Place the lemon slices on the breasts. Baste the chicken with the pan juices.

Place the skillet in a 350°F oven for 15 minutes or until juices run clear behind the wings.

Place the chicken breasts on warm plates. Deglaze the skillet with chicken stock and lemon juice. Spoon pan sauce over chicken.

To make the squash purée, place the quartered squash in a roasting pan. Add about ½ inch of water to the pan. Drizzle with olive oil and sprinkle with salt and pepper.

Cover and bake at 350°F until tender, about 20 minutes.

Pass the squash through a ricer or purée in a processor. Mix in the orange juice and butter. Adjust seasoning with salt and pepper. Add butternut squash to each plate and serve immediately.

MAI'S RESTAURANT

MIDTOWN
3403 MILAM STREET
(713) 520-5300
WWW.MAISHOUSTON.COM
CHEF/OWNER: MAI NGUYEN
OWNER: ANNA PHAM

You will not find more welcoming restaurateurs than Mai Nguyen and her daughter Anna. Mai runs the kitchen, while Anna works the front of house. Both do expert jobs. For any restaurant to survive thirty years is quite an accomplishment, but for a Vietnamese restaurant this is remarkable, considering the lack of adventurous dining thirty years ago. Mai's is a landmark in Houston that Mai's mother opened in 1978; everyone knows of it and most have eaten there at one time or another. After a devastating fire in 2010,

Mai and Anna rebuilt with the support of the entire community. The new space is bustling and busy, but the food comes out of the kitchen effortlessly and authentically Vietnamese.

For many restaurants "authentic" is a cliché, but Mai's is the real deal. Here you are presented the true flavors of Vietnam with no Westernization. Accompanying a bowl of hot and sour soup brimming with vegetables and plump shrimp, topped with crisp fried shallots is an herb rarely found on other Vietnamese salad plates, *tiá tô*. They call it lemon mint, but it is actually perilla. The *banh xeo* is a coconut milk-based crêpe stuffed with pork, shrimp, and sprouts, and when portions are wrapped in lettuce leaves with a bouquet of fresh herbs, it is heavenly in its combination of textures and flavors. The *lau ka* is a spicy hot pot of catfish with a perfect assemblage of Vietnamese spices. This is not a standard pho restaurant.

If you have room for dessert, go for the warm banana in coconut custard with tapioca pearls and peanuts, *Che Chuoi*. This will open your eyes to a whole new world of what dessert can be. For a most refreshing and unusual (by American standards) dessert, try the *Che 3 Mau*, shaved ice with sweetened three beans and thick coconut milk. It is not possible to put your spoon down until the glass is empty.

GARLIC BEEF

SERVES 4

Tenderloin, while very lean and tender, does not have as much flavor as do marbled cuts of meat. Consider using prime grade rib eye for a special occasion.

2 pounds beef tenderloin, cut into 1-inch cubes
½ cup (and more for glazing) oyster sauce
2 tablespoons soy sauce
1 tablespoon black pepper
1 tablespoon garlic powder
2 tablespoons nuoc mau (Vietnamese caramel sauce)
1 teaspoon salt
Peanut oil
1 onion, sliced thin
1 red bell pepper, seeded, membrane removed and
    sliced thin
2 jalapeños, sliced thin (remove seeds and membrane
    to control spiciness)
2 roasted garlic cloves
2 green onions, sliced into 2-inch segments,
    including white stems and greens
Romaine lettuce leaves for garnish
Ripe tomato slices for garnish
Red onion slices for garnish
4 garlic cloves, sliced thin
¼ cup peanut oil
2 cups cooked jasmine rice

Marinate the tenderloin cubes in the oyster sauce, soy sauce, pepper, garlic powder, nuoc mau, and salt for at least 48 hours.

Heat wok or large skillet over high heat. Add some peanut oil and when hot, toss in the marinated beef. Shake pan or stir to brown the meat on all sides, adding additional oyster sauce to glaze the beef cubes a rich caramelized brown color.

Add the onion, bell pepper, jalapeños, and roasted garlic. Add additional oyster sauce for glazing.

Place lettuce, tomatoes, and red onion on serving plates. Add portions of sautéed beef to each plate.

Fry the sliced garlic in peanut oil until crisp but not burned. Pour over the beef. Add a timbale of rice and serve immediately.

MARK'S AMERICAN CUISINE

MONTROSE
1658 WESTHEIMER ROAD
(713) 523-3800
WWW.MARKS1658.COM
CHEF/OWNER: MARK COX

Many food writers have referred to Mark's, housed in a renovated 1920s brick church, as a religious dining experience. The setting is Gothic and the atmosphere is subdued. The soaring arched ceiling absorbs errant noise, and the lighting is soft and welcoming. In spite of its reputation for outstanding food and service, this restaurant was conceived to be a neighborhood place, a restaurant where regulars come to dine, and not just a special occasion destination. Service is impeccable, with just the right amount of friendliness to make you feel relaxed. Chef and owner Mark Cox is dedicated to his employees, and his employees are dedicated to making your dining experience an exceptional one.

The food can be described as Modern American, where Chef Cox is not afraid to borrow from other cultures' flavor profiles, but is grounded in traditional American foods. Chef Cox brings excellent credentials to his eponymous restaurant. He is a graduate of the CIA in New York, did a stint at the Greenbrier in West Virginia, learned his trade at the Four Seasons in Washington DC, and polished his skills at Tony's, one of Houston's most famous eateries. Some of today's chefs adhere to strictly local produce and commodities, but, with overnight delivery from almost anywhere in the world, Mark seeks out the best, regardless of location. As an example, he flies in fresh Onset Bay oysters from Massachusetts, known for their plump, sweet flesh and salty overtone. He roasts them in their shell and tops them with a ragout of crabmeat, shrimp, and leeks. For textural contrast and as a bonus, he crowns this with a delicately fried oyster.

Chef Cox is playful with preparation and offers an ingredient cooked two ways, each yielding a different aspect to the ingredient. Hudson Valley foie gras is offered as a torchon, wrapped in cloth and slowly poached, and as a pan-seared slice for contrast. The former produces a pâté-like product, with a desirable metallic taste and spreadable texture, while the latter preparation forms a silken, barely held together buttery mass that melts in your mouth. Duck breast is seared and served rosy pink, with crisp skin, and rests on top of a slice of cured duck breast with the texture and taste of delicate ham. Prime rib is paired with short rib and the short rib is prepared in the manner of *sous vide* (slowly poached in a vacuum bag over very low heat), which brings out an intense brisket or "pot roast" flavor. The prime rib is grilled over coals, enhancing the steak flavor of the beef.

To intensify aroma, the capellini with Parmesan and truffle cream is served with a glass dome to cover until set in front of you. When the cover is removed, an over-powering truffle essence invades your senses. If that were not enough, fresh white truffle is immediately shaved over the pasta for total sensory immersion.

Sashimi Tuna & Soba Noodles with Jicama Slaw

SERVES 2

Some ingredients may be difficult to obtain, such as *yuzu shibori* juice. It can be ordered online, but a mixture of equal parts orange, lemon, and tangerine juices can substitute. If you can't find opal basil, use Thai basil, another purple basil, or the common green basil.

For the sashimi and noodles:

1 (2-inch) piece fresh ginger with skin, roughly chopped
8 ounces packaged soba noodles
½ cup soy sauce
½ tablespoon sesame oil
½ tablespoon yuzu shibori juice (see above)
½ tablespoon mirin
2 tablespoons black and white sesame seeds
¼ teaspoon Thai fish sauce
¼ cup sweet chile sauce
1 tablespoon opal basil vinegar (infuse rice vinegar with chopped basil leaves)
½ tablespoon tamarind purée
8 ounces sashimi-grade ahi tuna, cut into small dice

For the jicama slaw (makes 2 cups):

¼ teaspoon sambal
1 tablespoon Thai fish sauce
1 tablespoon light soy sauce
1 tablespoon white soy sauce
½ tablespoon yuzu juice (see above)
½ teaspoon sesame oil
½ tablespoon sugar in the raw
Juice of ½ orange
Juice of ½ lime
2 tablespoons olive oil
¼ small jicama, peeled, fine julienne
½ small baihon, fine julienne
1 large carrot, peeled, fine julienne
1 tablespoon finely sliced mint
1 tablespoon finely sliced cilantro

To serve:

½ ruby red grapefruit, sectioned
½ bunch green onions, finely sliced
1 bunch opal basil, finely sliced (see above)
10 cherry tomatoes, halved
Cilantro sprigs
1 avocado, peeled, cut into small dice
Black and white sesame seeds

Bring 2 quarts water to a boil. Add the chopped ginger and noodles and cook al dente. Drain the noodles and allow to cool. Reserve.

Mix the soy sauce, sesame oil, *yuzu* juice, mirin, sesame seeds, fish sauce, sweet chile sauce, vinegar, and tamarind purée together. Toss in the tuna and allow to marinate, refrigerated 10 minutes.

For the slaw, whisk the sambal, fish sauce, both soy sauces, yuzu, sesame oil, sugar, orange and lime juices, and olive oil together to form a dressing for the jicama slaw.

Toss the jicama, baihon, carrot, mint, and cilantro together. Add the dressing and toss gently. Refrigerate until needed.

Toss the soba noodles with the jicama slaw.

Place portions of tuna on the plates. Top with soba noodles/slaw. Garnish each plate with grapefruit sections, green onions, opal basil, cherry tomato halves, cilantro, and avocado. Sprinkle sesame seeds over and serve.

Max's Wine Dive

WASHINGTON AVENUE
4720 WASHINGTON AVENUE
(713) 880-8737
WWW.MAXSWINEDIVE.COM
CHEF: MICHAEL PELLEGRINO
OWNERS: LASCO ENTERPRISES

The atmosphere can be raucous here at Max's, but in a good way. The noise level is intentional and infectious. The owners, Jerry and Laura Lasco (and son Max), wanted to re-create their favorite "dive" in Manhattan, a bar that was boisterous, narrow, brick-walled, and just a bit seedy. There is nothing seedy about Max's, though. The food is described by Chef Michael Pellegrino as "gourmet comfort food." Imagine French toast soaked in crème brulée custard before grilling or a burger made from ground Kobe beef, triple crème brie, surrounded by a homemade brioche bun with garnishes of homemade pickled jalapeños and organic Bibb lettuce.

Their popular Max 'n Cheese appetizer is macaroni and cheese taken to a new level with the infusion of truffles in a cheesy combination of Gruyere, provolone, and Parmigiana Reggiano. There's meat loaf, but with a red curry sauce replacing the requisite red ketchup, potpie with lobster instead of chicken. Chef Pellegrino was born to cook, as he recalls wanting to be a chef ever since he can remember. It shows as his food is luscious, comforting, approachable, and never silly. His updates on the traditional are smart, thought through, and executed with superior skill.

But there is more to Max's Wine Dive—the wine. This fabulous restaurant is also a retail wine shop. You can purchase any wine off the list at prices approaching your favorite retail shop. Enjoy a reasonably priced glass of wine from their extensive menu with dinner and leave with a bottle.

Max 'n Cheese

SERVES 2–4

Cavatappi means corkscrew and nicely describes the spiral tubes of pasta. In some ways they are double elbow macaroni, so that may be the best substitute, easily found in every market. Cavatappi is also called tortiglione and cellantani.

⅓ cup béchamel sauce

2 tablespoons heavy cream

5 dry ounces cavatappi pasta, cooked al dente, or other interestingly shaped pasta

½ teaspoon truffle oil

2 ounces grated Parmesan cheese

2 ounces grated white cheddar

2 ounces grated gruyere

Salt and pepper

Juice of ¼ lime

1 cup buttered dry bread crumbs

In a sauté pan add the béchamel and heavy cream. Cook over low heat until bubbles form in the center. Stir in the cooked pasta, truffle oil, and the 3 cheeses.

Allow the mixture to simmer, stirring occasionally, until the chesses have melted into a sauce.

Season with salt and pepper to taste and stir in the lime juice.

Place the pasta into a casserole and top with buttered bread crumbs. Place under a broiler until golden. Serve immediately.

CRÈME BRULÉE FRENCH TOAST

SERVES 4

This may be the ultimate French toast recipe. It is unique in that, rather than an egg wash or dipping liquid that is cold and uses raw eggs, a cooked custard is made to bathe the brioche bread.

1 quart heavy cream
2 cups sugar
1 vanilla bean, split open lengthwise
9 egg yolks
Clarified butter
1 loaf brioche, sliced 1½ inches thick
Syrup or preserves for service

Add the cream, 1 cup sugar, and the vanilla bean and the seeds scraped from the interior to a saucepan. Heat to a boil over medium heat.

Whisk the remaining sugar and the egg yolks in a large bowl until thick and pale.

Slowly whisk the hot cream mixture into the egg yolks, a little at a time. Allow this custard to cool.

Brush a nonstick skillet with clarified butter and place over medium-high heat.

Dip the brioche slices into the custard, allowing the bread to absorb as much liquid as possible, turning once. Add them to the pan, cooking a few slices at a time, 2 minutes on each side. Reserve the cooked toasts on a plate in a warm oven until all slices are cooked.

Serve at once with syrup or preserves of your choice.

Mockingbird Bistro

River Oaks
1985 Welch Street
(713) 533-0200
www.mockingbirdbistro.com
Chef/Owner: John Sheely

One definition of a bistro is an informal, small restaurant serving wine, a perfectly good description for the Mockingbird Bistro, named after the state bird of Texas. Meant as a River Oaks neighborhood venue to drop in for a glass of wine and an appetizer or to dine socially on simply prepared foods using impeccably fresh ingredients, Chef/Owner John Sheely has hit the mark.

The inviting bar wraps around the restaurant and invites one to sit and dine while enjoying a glass of wine or a cocktail. Look up and see the amazing chandeliers recovered from one of Houston's earliest fine dining spots, Sonny Look's Sirloin Inn. Chef Sheely understands flavor and does not muddle things up with complicated, multiple sauces or seasonings; the ingredients speak for themselves. Chef Sheely describes the food style as "Texas Provence," staying true to local produce, meats, and fish, and applying the principles of provincial cookery. Spring rabbit with olives, heirloom tomatoes, and a confit leg is quintessentially southern France inspired.

Bistro food, such as steak frites with a juicy, expertly grilled prime strip steak, is served with fried potatoes and aioli for dipping. Caramelized shallots accompany the dish and are slowly cooked and intensely sweet. Strawberry grouper (red hind) is perfectly cooked and rests atop a mélange of crawfish, haricots vert, and oyster mushrooms, with little else to cloud the inherent flavors of the ingredients. Save room for dessert, or drop in late for dessert and a fabulous pairing with wine, and do not miss the Granny Smith apple bread pudding with caramel sauce and cinnamon ice cream. *Magnifique!*

SLOW-BRAISED SHORT RIBS

SERVES 6

Beef short ribs are the anatomical equivalent to pork spare ribs, but are much meatier. They are cut several different ways depending on the style of dish and country of origin of the recipe. The English and Koreans cut them across the rib bones into thin strips, whereas in America they are most often separated by the bones, making thick ribs that thrive on low temperature and long cooking times.

2 tablespoons and additional olive oil

6 pounds meaty beef short ribs

Coarse salt and pepper

1 large onion, finely diced

1 medium carrot, peeled and finely chopped

1 celery stalk, finely chopped

12 whole garlic cloves, peeled

1 tablespoon dried herbes de Provence

2 cups red Zinfandel

2½ cups veal stock or beef broth

2 medium tomatoes, chopped with juice

1 bay leaf

Zest of 1 orange

Zest of 1 lemon

6 cups creamy polenta or garlic mashed potatoes for service

Preheat the oven to 325°F.

Heat 2 tablespoons olive oil in heavy large ovenproof pot over medium-high heat. Sprinkle ribs with coarse salt and pepper. Working in batches, add ribs to the pot and brown well, turning often, about 8 minutes per batch. Add additional olive oil as necessary. Remove the ribs as they finish browning to a large tray.

Pour off all but 2 tablespoons of drippings from the pot. Add the onion, carrot, and celery and cook over medium-low heat until vegetables are soft, stirring frequently, about 8 minutes.

Add the garlic and herbes de Provence and stir 1 minute. Add the wine and 2 cups of broth. Bring to boil over high heat, scraping the browned bits from the bottom of the pan.

Add the chopped tomatoes with juices and the bay leaf. Return ribs and any accumulated juices to pot. If needed, add enough water to pot to barely cover ribs. Bring to boil. Remove from the heat and add the orange and lemon zest.

Cover the pot tightly and transfer to the preheated oven. Bake until ribs are very tender, about 2 hours. This dish can be made 1 day ahead and reheated for service.

Serve with creamy polenta or garlic mashed potatoes.

MOLINA'S CANTINA

WASHINGTON AVENUE
4720 WASHINGTON AVENUE
(713) 862-0013
WWW.MOLINASRESTAURANTS.COM
CHEFS/OWNERS: MOLINA FAMILY

The Molina family has been serving Tex-Mex food to Houstonians for seventy years, so it's obvious that they are doing something right. A fine indicator of a quality restaurant is its employees, and many have been working for the Molina family for decades; several cooks have been there for more than twenty-five years. Tracing back three generations, the first of the Molinas to work in a restaurant was Grandpa in 1929 at the Old Monterrey. He opened the Mexico City Restaurant in 1941 and the family has been cooking tasty Mexican cuisine with a Texas flair ever since.

Some feel that the Molina family originated the style known as Tex-Mex. Regardless, the food quality is far above standard Tex-Mex fare. *Carnitas* are a good measure of a Mexican kitchen's abilities, as these pork cubes can easily be dry and overcooked or soggy and overstewed. Here they are perfect! Fork tender, juicy, and crisp on the surface, Molina's *carnitas* were so in demand that they had to be moved from a Friday special to a regular spot on the daily menu.

A nice touch to table service is the addition of house-made *escabeche* served alongside two salsas and warm, crisp tostados (tortilla chips) when you are seated. The carrot slices in the escabeche are still crisp, yet thoroughly pickled and spicy from the accompanying jalapeños. The avocado is celebrated here, and the guacamole is as good as it gets. Tomatillo green sauce is enhanced with avocado as well, making a typical sauce extraordinary. Molina's pays homage to its creative guests whenever they come up with tasty combinations not envisioned by the kitchen. When a guest, in an inspired moment, added some of his taco meat to the chile con queso, it launched a menu item called Jose's Dip. There's also Nancy Ames' Special Nachos, Berley's Burrito, and the C.W. Special.

As you peruse the menu, look for annotated items flagged with "since 1941," as these recipes haven't changed in seventy years. There are three locations in which to enjoy the best in Tex-Mex cooking—one on Washington Avenue, another on Westheimer (established in 1965), and their latest opening in Bellaire.

Cream of Poblano Soup with Roasted Corn & Sausage

SERVES 8

The poblano chile is most versatile with a unique, earthy flavor. It is the chile often stuffed for chile relleno. When allowed to ripen to red and then dried, it is the ancho chile, spicier and fruitier than when green. It is a base ingredient for mole sauces. When cut into strips and sautéed with onions, it becomes the garnish *rajas*.

4 ounces (½ cup) butter

⅓ cup flour

1 quart chicken stock

2¼ cups roasted, peeled, seeded, and
    puréed poblano peppers

1 quart heavy cream

¼ cup olive oil

1¼ cups diced yellow onion

8 poblano peppers, roasted, peeled,
    seeded, and diced

6 red bell peppers, roasted, peeled,
    seeded, and diced

6 ears roasted fresh corn, kernels removed

1 cup chopped fresh cilantro

⅓ cup fresh lime juice

Salt and pepper to taste

1¼ pounds jalapeño pork or chicken sausage links,
    cooked, sliced, and quartered

Melt butter in a large saucepan over medium heat. Add the flour and stir to form a roux. Cook 2 minutes.

Whisk in the chicken stock slowly, forming a smooth mixture. Add the puréed poblano peppers and reduce the heat to low. Simmer 15 to 20 minutes.

Add the heavy cream and cook an additional 10 minutes. Strain the soup base and return to the pot.

Add the olive oil to a large skillet and sauté the onions over medium heat for 1 minute. Add the diced poblanos, diced red peppers, and corn kernels. Cook until vegetables are soft, about 3 minutes.

Add the cilantro and lime juice.

Add the vegetable mixture to the soup base and simmer 5 minutes, stirring occasionally.

Season with salt and pepper.

Serve in individual bowls with pieces of sausage to garnish.

Monarch

Montrose/Museum District
5701 Main Street
(713) 527-1800
www.hotelzazahouston.com/houston-fine-dining
Chef: Adam West
Owner: Z Resorts

With a separate entrance and separate valet parking, you may not realize that Monarch is the restaurant of Hotel ZaZa, a boutique luxury hotel in the Museum District on the edge of Montrose. As with other hotels in Houston, their restaurant is more than just to service their guests; it's a venue of the residents of Houston as well. The ambiance of the restaurant and hotel is eclectic Deco, with exquisite black-and white photography including celebrity portraits of Dali, Rosalind Russell, and Marilyn Monroe decorating the walls. The inviting restaurant patio is covered by a giant palapa-like umbrella, with orange fairy lights strewn across the ceiling.

The menu at Monarch is also eclectic, in a good way. It allows their young and talented chef to appeal to the widest of audiences, a product of being associated with a hotel catering to world travelers. Chef West has learned well about flavor and quality. Often young chefs mistake quality for flavor or mask quality with too much flavor, but Chef has struck an important balance beyond his years. His style is not too simple but not too complicated, as seen in an appetizer of briefly cured yellowtail (hamachi), complemented with a slice of ripe jalapeño, lime juice, and a sprig of microgreens including cilantro. A chilled soup of *pequillo* peppers and ripe tomatoes with just a hint of toasted fennel seeds on top is just right.

Chef West can be playful in an intelligent way when he pairs seared foie gras with dried cherries poached in cherry Dr Pepper syrup, bringing a bit of Texas to an ingredient that pairs nicely with sweet elements. Joining fresh tarragon with shaved fennel and orange juice to accompany heirloom tomatoes is another example of his restrained hand. Updating a classic German schnitzel (a requirement on the menu by the owners of the hotel), an intense reduction of stock and roasted cippolini onions brings out the subtle flavor of veal without masking it.

RED PEPPER & ROASTED TOMATO GAZPACHO

SERVES 8

Gazpacho is an Andalusian cold soup made with raw vegetables, served during the sweltering summer months to refresh. Historically bread was a main component of this dish, but it has fallen out of favor over the centuries.

3 pounds Roma tomatoes, washed and quartered
1 tablespoon minced garlic
1 teaspoon chopped fresh basil
1 teaspoon chopped fresh oregano
2 tablespoons olive oil
3 red bell peppers, roasted, peeled, and seeded
8 ounces tomato juice
About 1 cup pure olive oil
Salt and pepper
Cucumber wedges for garnish

Toss the tomatoes, garlic, basil, oregano, and olive oil together and roast in a pan at 300°F for 1 hour, or until soft and well browned.

Add the contents of the roasting pan, the bell peppers, and tomato juice to a blender and purée until smooth. Add olive oil in a slow stream until desired consistency is reached. Season with salt and pepper. Chill thoroughly before serving.

Serve in chilled cocktail glasses garnished with cucumber wedges.

VEAL SCHNITZEL

SERVES 4

Wiener Schnitzel, or Viennese Schnitzel, is traditionally served in Austria without sauce, garnished simply with slices of lemon and accompanied with buttered potatoes or potato salad.

For the veal:

4 (6-ounce) veal cutlets
1 cup seasoned flour (seasoned with 1 teaspoon each garlic powder, onion powder, salt)
3 tablespoons peanut oil
4 cippolini onions, peeled and quartered
1 cup veal stock or beef broth
1 tablespoon butter
Dash of sherry vinegar
Salt and pepper

For the fingerling potatoes:

3 cups fingerling potatoes, quartered
¼ cup olive oil
1 teaspoon chopped fresh thyme
1 teaspoon chopped fresh rosemary
Coarse salt and fresh ground pepper

Dredge the veal in seasoned flour.

Heat a large skillet with the oil over medium heat and add the veal cutlets. Sauté 2 minutes on each side. Reserve the cutlets on a warm plate.

Drain most of the oil from pan, leaving the brown bits stuck to the pan. Add the cippolini onions and lightly sauté for 3 minutes over low heat.

Add the veal stock and scrape the bottom of the pan to loosen the browned bits. Reduce the volume by two-thirds over medium heat.

Stir in the butter and add the vinegar. Adjust seasoning with salt and pepper.

To make the potatoes, toss the fingerlings with the oil and fresh herbs.

Roast the seasoned potatoes, at 400°F until tender and golden brown, about 20 minutes.

Season with salt and pepper.

Pour sauce and onions over reserved veal cutlets and serve immediately with fingerling potatoes on the side.

Nino's / Vincent's / Grappino di Nino

Montrose (Neartown)
2817-2701 West Dallas Street
(713) 528-1008
www.ninos-vincents.com
Chef/Owner: Vincent Mandola

What started out as a small Italian restaurant named after Vincent Mandola's father has become a small mecca of fine Italian dining with three unique venues. Nino's is comfortable and intimate, keeping the character and wooden floors and paneling of the early-20th-century neighborhood market and home that was remodeled. When the property next door became available, it started as a sandwich shop and slowly expanded to a large, modern dining facility with a wood-burning pizza oven and rotisserie. The third addition is a venue for parties, outdoor socializing, and nibbling on luscious appetizers.

Each has its own feel and menu, but there are a few menu items that are so popular that they are served in each—Veal Vincent, Snapper Nino, and Scampi alla Griglia. The veal is Parmesan-crusted scallops of veal in a delicate lemon-butter sauce. Gulf snapper is perfectly sautéed with mushrooms and lump crabmeat, and the sweet shrimp are

served in shell but split open like miniature lobster tails, served with a sauce of white wine, garlic, and butter. This provides the intense flavor of cooking shrimp in shell, without the mess of having to dig out the delicate meat.

Not on the menu but available to those in the know on Thursday is succulent and meaty osso bucco, topped with rich tomato sauce. The house-baked bread is perfect for mopping up all of the plates' sauces just mentioned. The most popular and famous dish served at Vincent's must be the rotisserie chicken with skin begging to be removed and eaten immediately. Its flavor is delicate, juicy, and rich, with a bit of smokiness. It should be noted that the chicken can be ordered to go, whole, and is a bargain. However, you can purchase the chicken at one of their convenient to-go Pronto stores across the city.

Dessert is not an afterthought, and the banana split pie has been on the menu since day one. However, the cannoli are maybe the best anywhere—including New York City!

SNAPPER NINO

SERVES 6

Almost any delicate fish fillet can be used in this easy-to-prepare and versatile dish. The original recipe called for boneless trout, which would be an excellent substitute.

⅓ cup extra-virgin olive oil

6 (8-ounce) snapper fillets

Salt and pepper

2 eggs, beaten

1 cup sliced mushrooms

½ cup chopped roasted red peppers

6 ounces lump crabmeat, picked over for bits of shell and cartilage

3 ounces (6 tablespoons) unsalted butter

Juice of 2 lemons

Dry white wine

Heat the olive oil in a large sauté pan over medium heat. Season the fillets with salt and pepper and then dip into beaten egg, allowing excess egg to drain off.

Place the coated fish in the pan and cook 2 to 3 minutes on each side until golden brown. Place on warm plates.

Add the mushrooms, peppers, and crabmeat to the sauté pan. Add the butter, lemon juice, and a splash of white wine. Sauté until the mushrooms are cooked and the crab is heated through, about 3 minutes.

Top the fillets with the crab mixture. Serve immediately.

VEAL VINCENT

SERVES 4

When battering and frying, do as the professionals do. Have one hand for dredging in dry ingredients and the other for wet. In this way you avoid breading your fingers rather than the food.

8 (3-ounce) slices veal from the leg
½ cup flour
¾ cup grated Parmesan cheese
⅓ cup olive oil
2 eggs, beaten
8 artichoke hearts, packed in water,
    drained, warmed
4 ounces (½ cup) melted butter
Juice of 1 lemon

Pound the veal lightly until approximately ⅛ inch thick.

Mix the flour and cheese together.

Heat the olive oil in a large skillet over medium heat.

Dredge the veal scallops in the cheese mixture and then dip in the beaten egg. Coat the veal scallops on both sides with the cheese mixture, pressing firmly to adhere.

Carefully place the veal in hot oil. Cook until golden brown, about 2 minutes per side. Stir together the melted butter and lemon juice.

Place 2 veal scallops on each plate. Add artichoke hearts and drizzle with butter and lemon juice mixture. Serve immediately.

Food festivals are a great part of any city's food scene, and Houston's **Original Greek Festival,** in its forty-fifth year, has been a favorite October way to dance like Zorba and eat Greek delicacies homemade by the parishioners of the Annunciation Greek Orthodox Cathedral. The selection of Greek favorites includes souvlaki, gyros, tiropita, spanakopita, dolmades, Greek salad, and pastitsio, as well as baklava, kourambiedes, and loukoumades for the sweet tooth in all of us. The festival lasts four days, Thursday through Sunday, and includes dance exhibitions, live Greek music, and movies (yes, *Zorba the Greek* is a perennial favorite). For details go to www.greek festival.org.

When you see *original* in any title, you can be sure that there is at least one other that came after. **Houston Greek Fest** is held in May by the parishioners of St. Basil the Great Greek Orthodox Church. You'll find many of the same Greek specialty foods. For information, visit www.houstongreekfest.com.

Celebrate the **Thai New Year** in April at Wat Buddhavas, Houston's Thai temple, and learn about Thai culture and enjoy delicious Thai food. The temple also sponsors a festival in October/November, **Loi Krathong, the Candlelight Floating Festival,** celebrating the end of the rainy season in Thailand. In Thailand boats and small floats in the shape of lotus flowers containing candles, incense, and flowers are sent down the swollen rivers and streams; in Houston a ceremonial pond is constructed to which participants bring their handmade small floats decorated with flowers and lit candles. Fabulous food is served from booths across the property.

The Italian Cultural and Community Center sponsors its three-day **Festa Italiana** annually, in October, on the grounds of the University of St. Thomas. It has grown from a modest fifteen booths in 1978 to Houston's largest ethnic festival. As food is central to the culture, it is central to this festival. In the Taste of Italy Pavilion, there are wine tastings and pairings with food, cooking demonstrations, and lots of sampling. Food concessions offer fantastic homemade delicacies such as Italian sausages, meatball sandwiches, pasta, and pizza. Italian desserts, if you can make room, include Italian water ices, gelato, cannoli, and delicate cookies. Get involved by joining the competitive pasta-eating contest or the grape-stomping contest. There's a bocce tournament for those practitioners and loads of activities for the kids.

Ooh La La Dessert Boutique

Katy
20155 Park Row
(281) 492-6166
www.oohlalasweets.com
Chef/Owner: Vanessa O'Donnell

Vanessa O'Donnell's mom owned a gift shop when she was growing up. One section had French items and a model of the Eiffel Tower with a sign affixed declaring "Ooh La La." Vanessa told her mom that someday, when she owned a shop of her own, that's what she'd name it. Vanessa is the owner and pastry chef of Ooh La La Dessert Boutique, one of the Houston area's most delicious and successful dessert bakeries. Her display cases must be cleaned of palm prints continuously as every kid who enters seems magnetically drawn to the windows revealing row after row of jumbo cupcakes piled high with frosting.

There's a carrot cake cupcake topped with cream cheese frosting, Pretty in Pink cupcakes with pink sprinkles atop cream cheese frosting above festively pink cake. The top seller is the red velvet cupcake with vanilla frosting. The list includes more than a dozen varieties, some of them rotating with seasons and holidays. There are daily cupcake flavors as well, so don't miss Thursday's Cherry Limeade cupcake with cherry cake, lime buttercream, and a cherry on top with candied lime peel.

But kids of all ages do not live by cupcakes alone. There are pies, cookies, cakes, cheesecakes, dessert bars, and pastries. The lemon bars will bring you back in time to Grandma's kitchen. You'd better have a glass of milk handy to tackle the chewy chocolate cookie, the size of a salad plate and loaded with walnuts and pure chocolate. There's a build-your-own cake menu where you select from about eighteen types of cake, then choose a filling of fresh berries, mousses of every imaginable flavor, custards and curds, or buttercreams.

If you make it that far you are ready for icings—myriad buttercreams, cream cheese frosting (lemon, chocolate, or vanilla), or ganache. If none of this interests you, try a delicious pie. Everything in the shop can be bought by the slice or whole. Eat in with some great coffee or take it home.

Hummingbird Cake

MAKES 2 (10-INCH) ROUND CAKE LAYERS

This recipe makes a very moist cake and can be baked in loaf pans or as cupcakes. While rich enough to skip the luscious frosting, cupcakes are always better with a decadent icing!

For the cake:

2 cups flour
1¾ cups granulated sugar
½ teaspoon salt
½ teaspoon cinnamon
½ teaspoon baking soda
3 eggs
1 teaspoon vanilla extract
9 ounces (1 cup plus 1 tablespoon) butter, melted, cooled
1¼ cups crushed pineapple
3 cups mashed bananas

For the cream cheese frosting:

12 ounces (1½ cups) softened unsalted butter
1 pound powdered (confectioners') sugar
1½ tablespoons vanilla bean paste
    (or 1 tablespoon vanilla extract)
1 pound softened cream cheese

Combine all dry ingredients in mixing bowl and mix together by hand.

Add the eggs and vanilla to the melted butter. Whisk until completely incorporated.

Add the egg mixture to the dry ingredients, using a rubber spatula, mixing until smooth and uniform. Add the pineapple and bananas to combine. Do not overmix.

Divide the batter into 2 (10-inch) springform pans that have been greased and floured.

Bake at 350°F for 40 minutes or until golden brown and set in the center. Allow to cool thoroughly before frosting.

Cut each cake in half horizontally to form layers.

To make the icing, beat the butter with half of the powdered sugar until smooth. Stir in the vanilla bean paste.

Add the cream cheese and remaining powdered sugar and beat until light and fluffy.

Frost each cake with cream cheese icing and refrigerate until needed.

Original Ninfa's on Navigation

2nd Ward
2704 Navigation Boulevard
(713) 228-1175
www.ninfas.com
Chef: Alex Padilla
Owner: Legacy Restaurants

What would Tex-Mex cuisine be without fajitas? You can thank Maria Ninfa Rodriguez Laurenzo for placing grilled skirt steak inside a tortilla and popularizing the dish to its current fame. A native of the Rio Grande Valley, Ninfa started in the food business by selling wholesale pizza dough and tortillas in 1948 with her husband, Tommy Laurenzo. She began selling tacos *al carbon* in her small tortilla bakery in Houston in 1973, which is still the site of Ninfa's original restaurant.

Located in the Second Ward on Navigation Boulevard, dining there is the reason for being in this neighborhood for now. There are hints of this strip becoming a new hot spot for dining, but that is years away. Service is impeccable and servers have been with Ninfa's for up to twenty years, proudly serving award-winning Mexican food. Houstonians have been coming faithfully to dine on delicious Tex-Mex favorites, cooked from scratch with the finest ingredients for almost forty years. Many eat there several times per week.

With such a loyal following, it may seem daring and questionable to bring in a young chef trained at Boulevard in San Francisco to vitalize the menu. They did exactly that and it is a success. Chef Padilla has kept the best of the traditional menu and added his own twist to modern Tex-Mex. In addition to finding traditional *platos Mexicanos* (combination plates of tamales, enchiladas, tacos, etc.), grilled salmon over chorizo grits, or a chile relleno stuffed with crawfish and fresh garbanzo beans can be found on Chef's specials menu.

PORK ROAST YUCATAN STYLE

COCHINITA PIBIL

SERVES 6

Cochinita means baby pig and the Mayans of Yucatan would prepare this dish that way, with the piglet wrapped in banana leaves and cooked in the ground with hot rocks. Rather than a mixture of citrus juices as called for in this recipe, the juice of the Seville or bitter orange would be used. For an authentic dish, seek out these oranges and replace the juice mixture below with it.

For the pork:

¼ cup coarse salt
⅓ cup black pepper
1 tablespoon ground cumin (comino)
5 pounds pork butt
½ cup red wine vinegar
Juice of 1½ grapefruits
Juice of 2 oranges
Juice of 3 limes
Juice of 3 lemons
1½ cups pineapple juice
¼ cup roasted garlic cloves
1 cup achote paste
2 medium tomatoes, roasted, peeled, and seeded
⅓ cup dried oregano
Salt and pepper
1 banana leaf
2 small bay leaves
1 onion, sliced
½ pound tomatoes, sliced

For the pickled onions:

2 red onions, peeled and sliced in thin rings
Juice of 2 oranges
Juice of 2 limes
Juice of 2 lemons
⅓ cup grapefruit juice
2 tablespoons olive oil

½ tablespoon coarse salt
Red wine vinegar to cover
2 tablespoons sugar

For the fried plantains:

Vegetable oil
3 firm-ripe plantains, about 1½ pounds,
    peeled and sliced into ¼-inch rounds
Coarse salt

To serve:

3 cups cooked rice
Mexican crema (or crème fraîche)

Combine the salt, pepper, and cumin together in a small bowl. Rub all sides of the pork roast with this mixture.

In a large hot sauté pan, brown all sides of the pork.

In a blender add the vinegar, the citrus and pineapple juices, the roasted garlic, achote paste, and roasted tomatoes. Purée until smooth. Stir in the oregano and season to taste with salt and pepper.

Place the pork butt on the banana leaf and top with the bay leaves, sliced onions, and tomatoes. Season the top with salt.

Wrap the banana leaf around the pork and cover with aluminum foil. Roast at 350°F for about 3 hours, until the meat is tender. Remove the pork butt from the hot pan and allow to cool, wrapped.

To make the onions, add them to a nonreactive saucepan with the citrus juices, olive oil, and salt. Add enough red wine vinegar to completely cover the onions.

Bring the mixture to a boil and then remove from the heat. Stir in the sugar and allow to cool.

Transfer the onions and liquid to a glass jar or plastic container and store, refrigerated, until needed.

For the plantains, heat about 1 inch of oil in a heavy-bottomed skillet over medium heat until just below the smoking point.

Carefully add the plantains to the oil, turning occasionally, until they are a golden brown, about 4 minutes.

Remove with a slotted spoon and drain on paper towels. Sprinkle with salt.

Unwrap the pork roast and cut into 6 equal portions. Serve with pickled onions, fried plantains, a timbale of rice, and a dollop of Mexican crema.

Ouisie's Table

River Oaks
3939 San Felipe Drive
(713) 528-2264
www.ouisiestable.com
Executive Chef/Owner: Elouise Adams Jones

Charming. A perfect word to describe so much of what Ouisie's Table is all about. Charming describes the warm feel of a Southern country home that is the interior and decor of this icon of Houston dining. The main dining room is tall and expansive, yet warm and friendly at the same time. A favorite dining room is the "porch," sun-drenched with tall windows and filtered light, as you would imagine a sunroom in an antebellum mansion in the South.

"Charming" describes the owner and executive chef, Elouise Adams Jones. It is her spirit that is captured in every aspect of this great dining venue. She is responsible for the decor and the quality of the host and waitstaff, not to mention the food. Nothing escapes her touch. At home she will tinker with a recipe, develop ideas, create inspirational combinations of flavors, and then bring them to the restaurant for kitchen development, soon to appear on the menu.

Charming is the menu itself, a combination of home, Southern, American, and regional influences. Her grandmother, Lucy, passed down some fine recipes that became standards of the menu. Brandied oysters are Lucy's recipe and should not be missed. Be sure to ask for extra bread to soak up the luscious liquid left after downing the oysters in rapid succession. Nestled next to a considerable portion of chicken-fried steak is Lucy's delicate, rich corn pudding, which could stand on its own as a featured dish.

Also on this same plate are some of the best mashed potatoes outside your grandma's kitchen. These are honest potatoes, not passed through a ricer or sieve, but actually mashed with bits of firm potato distributed carefree.

The fried Gulf Coast oysters are succulent, sweet, and tender, contrasting perfectly with a crisp cornmeal coating. House-made jalapeño tartar sauce is the perfect complement as is their red sauce. Greens define Southern cooking and their quality separates the truly good Southern cooks. Under a fillet of perfectly cooked red snapper is a bed of greens and cabbage that have been steamed in a lime-ginger broth that elevates the snapper to new heights. Mustard greens, cooked just right, are tangy and still resemble a leafy green. These are found on the chicken-fried steak plate along with black-eyed peas. A bit of Texas is represented by the bacon-wrapped smoked quail and wild boar sausage, both excellent, and are accompanied by locally grown Brussels sprouts. Save room for dessert. It will be hard to make up your mind between the wonderful icebox lemon pie, dark chocolate cake, *tres leches* cake, and assorted custards.

OUISIE'S SPLENDID SPUD

SERVES 2

An alternate presentation, one that Ouisie's does occasionally, is to use individual C size red potatoes rather than slices of larger potatoes. Trim the bottoms of each to allow them to stand up and cut the tops to accept the toppings.

2 small California white potatoes wrapped in foil
    and baked until tender
¼ cup extra-virgin olive oil
Freshly ground black pepper and sea salt
2 large garlic cloves, peeled and sliced paper thin
Zest of 1 lemon
2 scallions chopped fine, including some greens
½ cup crème fraîche or sour cream
2 ounces salmon roe
2 ounces smoked salmon sliced into
    ½-inch-wide strips
1 lemon wedge, seeds removed, cut thick enough
    to squeeze it
6 sprigs flat-leaf parsley
6 nice leaves baby arugula

When the potatoes are cool, slice off the ends and discard. Cut each potato into 3 medallions.

Place 3 medallions on each plate slightly separated. Brush each generously with olive oil and sprinkle with fresh pepper and salt.

Place a few garlic slices on top of each medallion and distribute the lemon zest over the garlic. Add some chopped scallions.

Spoon teaspoon-size dollops of crème fraîche in the center of each potato, leaving a soft peak.

Top each with salmon roe.

Place smoked salmon strips around the plates. Squeeze lemon juice over the salmon. Garnish with parsley and arugula. Finish with grindings of black pepper around the border of the plates.

FRIED OYSTERS

SERVES 4

The clever use of both cornmeal and corn flour, a powdery grind of cornmeal known as masa in Mexican cuisine, gives a nice crunch to the coating when fried. Allowing the coated oysters to rest before frying ensures the coating adheres to the slippery oysters.

For the oysters:

Canola oil for deep-frying (about 1 quart)
4 dozen shucked oysters, drained
1 quart buttermilk
½ cup corn flour
1½ cups cornmeal
1 teaspoon salt
1 teaspoon fresh ground pepper

For the red sauce (makes about 2½ cups):

2 cups ketchup
2 tablespoons fresh lemon juice
2 tablespoons Worcestershire sauce
1 tablespoon Tabasco sauce
1 tablespoon prepared horseradish
Pinch salt

Heat the oil in a deep fryer or deep pan to 370°F.

Place the oysters in a shallow dish with the buttermilk.

Mix the corn flour with the cornmeal, salt, and pepper. Dredge the oysters in this mixture, carefully coating each oyster. Remove them to a sheet pan to rest 1 minute.

Fry at 370°F until crispy and brown, about 2 minutes. Fry in batches and do not crowd them.

Drain on paper towels.

To make the red sauce, mix all ingredients together. Adjust spiciness with Tabasco and horseradish. Serve the oysters with red sauce on the side.

PHILIPPE RESTAURANT AND LOUNGE

GALLERIA/UPTOWN
1800 POST OAK BOULEVARD
(713) 439-1000
WWW.PHILIPPEHOUSTON.COM
CHEF/OWNER: PHILIPPE SCHMIT

On the edge of the Galleria, a neighborhood known for fine dining and great shopping, a gem of a restaurant is not to be missed. Philippe Schmit, owner and chef of Philippe Restaurant and Lounge, tirelessly oversees every detail of the exquisitely prepared food sent from the kitchen. The two-story restaurant houses a cozy lounge on the first floor and a dining room flooded with natural light on the second floor. The second floor is spacious and welcoming; the decor is restrained and classy. Service is attentive and friendly without being overbearing.

The food has a definite French foundation without fussiness or formality, and prices are remarkably reasonable considering the quality and care placed into every recipe. Philippe makes exquisitely flavored dishes that are not pretentious and are familiar to the American and Texan palate. There is a passion for quality and flavor and honesty in his approach to seasoning and taste. The food is so good that you can taste the dish in your mouth by the aromas rising from the plate set in front of you.

The lobster bisque is the distilled essence of all that makes lobster so desirable. Rather than a cream-based bisque, this soup relies on the stock itself to provide richness. In the center resides the most ethereal quenelle imaginable, light as air but never falling apart. His passion was born at an early age as Philippe recalls peering down

into the cellar kitchen of Maison Troisgros, gazing at the orchestrated fury of this three-star restaurant in his hometown of Roanne. He says that he knew that was to be his passion as he grew. He learned well from his mentor, Alain Dutournier, and as apprentice to Jean-Michel Diot. When Houston's Hotel Derek was sold and their restaurant Bistro Moderne closed, Philippe Schmit decided to stay in Houston, which was a very good thing for the Houston food scene.

Warm Goat Cheese & Potato Salad

Petatou

Serves 2

A simple vinaigrette can be made by stirring some prepared mustard into vinegar and then slowly whisking in some oil. Dijon or spicy mustard will give dimension to the vinaigrette as will wine or herb-flavored vinegars. Use three parts oil to one part vinegar.

2 small Yukon Gold potatoes

1 tablespoon shallots

½ cup prepared vinaigrette

2 tablespoons chives

1 teaspoon fresh thyme

1 tablespoon chopped black olives

Salt and black pepper

1 egg yolk

2 teaspoons water

2 teaspoons white wine

½ cup heavy cream

2 teaspoons fresh rosemary

4 ounces crumbled fresh goat cheese

Boil the potatoes in salted water until tender. Allow to cool. Cut into ½-inch slices.

Toss the cooled potatoes with the shallots, ⅓ cup of the prepared vinaigrette, the chives, thyme, and olives. Allow to stand 30 minutes. Adjust seasoning with salt and pepper.

Whisk the egg yolk with the water and wine over simmering water until thickened. Allow to cool.

Whisk the cream into the egg mixture and beat until soft peaks form. Fold in the rosemary. Adjust seasoning with salt and pepper.

Arrange slices of potato salad in a 3-inch ring in the center of each plate. Spread with goat cheese. Remove the rings.

Top with whipped cream mixture and place under a broiler until just golden.

Drizzle with remaining vinaigrette and serve immediately.

CRISPY RICE PAPER SALMON

SERVES 4

Rice papers or wrappers can be purchased at most Asian markets. They are the skins used in spring rolls, which become pliable (bend without breaking) and then soft (limp, shapeless) when soaked in warm water. The best method is to dip them quickly into the water, waiting until just pliable.

For the salmon:

4 ounces cooked broccoli florets
4 ounces basil leaves, blanched
¼ cup olive oil
2 ounces grated Parmesan cheese
¼ cup pine nuts
8 rice papers
4 (6-ounce) salmon fillets, from thickest part of salmon, cut into strips about 2 inches wide
2 egg yolks, beaten
Oil for sautéing

For the squash medley:

½ cup diced zucchini
½ cup diced yellow squash
½ cup diced butternut squash
½ cup diced tomato
⅓ cup olive oil
Zest and juice of 1 lemon
2 tablespoons sherry vinegar
Salt and pepper

Purée the cooked broccoli, basil leaves, olive oil, Parmesan, and pine nuts in a food processor to form a smooth paste (the pesto).

Soak the rice papers briefly in warm water to just make them pliable.

For each serving place a salmon fillet on 2 rice papers that overlap. Top with about 2 ounces of pesto. Roll, cigar fashion, and trim the ends to the edges of the salmon. Reserve.

When the rice papers have dried, brush them with egg yolk and sauté the salmon bundles in oil over medium heat on all sides to form a crisp shell, cooking the salmon medium rare, about 5 minutes.

To make the squash medley, blanch the zucchini, yellow squash, and butternut squash together in sufficient salted boiling water, about 2 minutes. Drain. Toss with the diced tomato.

Whisk the olive oil with the zest and juice of the lemon and the sherry vinegar to form an emulsion.

Stir the vinaigrette into the vegetables and allow to stand 1 minute. Add salt and pepper to taste. Serve or refrigerate and re-warm as needed.

Slice each salmon roll into 3 medallions and arrange on warm plates. Place vegetable medley to the side and serve immediately.

In 1956 postal worker Jeff McKissack started an homage to his favorite fruit, the orange. He transformed an East End lot into a maze of folk architecture and art and called it the Orange Show. Made from salvaged materials such as bricks, steel, and concrete, it incorporates gears, eighty tractor seats and eighty wagon wheels, and a multitude of cast-off things to make a wishing well, an oasis, and a soothing pond. There are mosaics and metal sculptures and figures brightly painted. Concrete owls and forty-five crafted metal birds keep an eye over plastic orange trees.

An exhibit of a chemical manufacturing factory called *Chemicals Left By the Sea,* made of used gas cylinders and toilet bowl floats, represents the body's use of nutrient chemicals from nutritious foods, especially oranges, grown on land that was left by the receding seas of primordial earth, nourishing crops for man to thrive upon. McKissack constructed this massive project by himself and worked on it until his death in 1980.

The Orange Show Center for Visionary Art was formed to preserve the Orange Show and the Beer Can House and preserves, promotes, and documents visionary art environments. It accepts donations and volunteers to run exhibits and maintain and upkeep these and future Houston treasures. The Orange Show can be experienced at 2402 Munger Street.

Pondicheri

Upper Kirby
2800 Kirby Drive, Suite B132
(713) 522-2022
www.pondichericafe.com
Chef/Owner: Anita Jaisinghani

Considered the epicenter of Houston, the neighborhood of Upper Kirby is a desirable location for most businesses—restaurants included—as it borders River Oaks, an exclusive neighborhood address. Here you will find the simply designed and welcoming Pondicheri.

Chef/Owner Anita Jaisinghani provides contemporary and authentic Indian street food in a space utilizing Indian fabrics, cooking pots, and tiles brought back from numerous travels to her homeland. The name of the restaurant is derivative of a favorite region she visited as a child in India, Pondicherry, and a place that is quite special in her heart. Authenticity is paramount to her recipes, and Chef Jaisinghani is adamant about making authentic Indian food approachable to all Houstonians. She wants everyone to "rethink Indian," to break away from preconceived notions garnered in so many Indian buffet restaurants found across the United States. Her spices are pure, fresh, and treated with respect. Seasoning is bold without being overbearing.

In addition Chef Jaisinghani has the heart of a baker and insists that all breads be baked from scratch in her kitchen, using her own starters rather than commercial yeasts. Pondicheri is open for breakfast (as well as lunch and dinner), so expect homemade brioche and loaf breads for her take on french toast and breakfast sandwiches, as well as flatbreads for roti's of lentils and spiced eggs. In addition to Pondicheri, Chef Jaisinghani also owns the hugely successful restaurant Indika (also featured, see page 78), a more traditional dining venue in Houston.

Chicken Vindaloo with Turmeric Rice

SERVES 4

Vindaloo is a dish prepared in the region of Goa, a former Portuguese colony in India on the west coast. It is known for being one of the spiciest Indian dishes and has a unique flavor profile with the addition of vinegar, not normally seen in this cuisine. In India the sign of good cooks is in their preparation of rice. Where most Asian cooked rice is sticky, Indian rice is judged by having each kernel independent of another, with no residual starch to hold it together. This is accomplished by extensive soaking and rinsing of raw rice, up to 24 hours, before cooking. The garnish may include a variety of vegetables and greens—or even pomegranate seeds as seen here.

For the chicken:

2 medium onions, sliced thin
3 tablespoons vegetable oil
3 garlic cloves, sliced thin
3 whole Serrano peppers
1 (2-inch) piece ginger, peeled, chopped
2 teaspoons ground turmeric
2 tablespoons chili powder
2 teaspoons ground cumin (comino)
2 teaspoons ground coriander seed
¼ cup corn oil
1 roasting chicken, about 4 pounds, cut up,
   skin removed
8 ounces coconut milk
3 tablespoons tomato purée
¼ cup balsamic vinegar
2 teaspoons garam masala
1 tablespoon salt

For the turmeric rice:

1½ cups raw (uncooked) basmati rice, rinsed 4 times,
   soaked at least 4 hours in warm water
2½ cups water
3 bay leaves
2 (3-inch) pieces stick cinnamon
1 teaspoon ground turmeric
2 tablespoons clarified butter
Salt
1½ cups green peas, freshly shucked or frozen
   (not canned)
1 tablespoon mustard seeds

Sauté the onions in oil over low heat until golden and aromatic. Add the sliced garlic and cook 2 minutes.

Add the cooked onions and garlic, the Serrano peppers, ginger, turmeric, chili powder, cumin, and coriander to a food processor and pulse to form a smooth paste.

In a large pot, heat the corn oil over medium heat. Sauté the chicken pieces, turning occasionally, until nicely browned on all sides.

Add the spice paste. Toss to coat and continue cooking for 10 minutes over medium-low heat, covering the pot after 5 minutes.

Add the coconut milk and tomato purée and simmer an additional 10 minutes over low heat.

Add the balsamic vinegar, garam masala, and salt. Toss to coat and turn off the heat. Allow to stand, covered, 2 minutes.

To cook the rice, mix the soaked and rinsed rice with 2½ cups water in a heavy-bottomed pot, the bay leaves, cinnamon sticks, turmeric, 1 tablespoon of clarified butter, and the salt. Bring to a boil, cover, and lower the heat to a simmer.

Cook without stirring for 7 to 8 minutes. Add the peas and continue to cook over low heat, until the water is absorbed, and the rice is cooked and fluffy.

In a small sauté pan, heat up the remaining clarified butter. When smoking, add the mustard seeds and let them pop and sizzle. Pour this over the rice and fold in gently with a spatula. Serve immediately in timbales with the chicken Vindaloo.

PREGO

WEST UNIVERSITY
2520 AMHERST STREET
(713) 529-2420
WWW.PREGO-HOUSTON.COM
CHEF/OWNER: JOHN WATT

The interior design of Prego captures the feel of an authentic Italian trattoria. The colors are neither vibrant nor subdued. The art on the walls gives the contemporary restaurant a splash of color that's just right, making it feel both relaxed and slightly upscale. The servers are knowledgeable and can guide you through the many delectable choices offered on the comprehensive menu. Chef/Owner John Watt is no newcomer to the restaurant business as the quality and flavor of his food demonstrates. Prior to opening this restaurant located in Rice Village (West U. or the Village), John left his mark on Backstreet Cafe and recently added a sister restaurant, Trevisio, in the Medical Center. Not only is Chef Watt a kitchen talent but he is also a jazz musician who has written jingles for commercials and is an accomplished artist in his own right. His food is well seasoned and packed with flavor, and the menu has both traditional favorites as well as modern Italian specialties.

Ten years ago, when John took over this space, few chefs were as demanding for organic produce, meats, and poultry as John, and he still relies on as many organic ingredients as he can get. The pastas are exceptional, and the assortment of handmade ravioli reflects all that is great about Prego. Some examples are wild mushroom with marsala sauce, earthy and intense, butternut squash with brown butter and sage, smoked duck with port wine sauce, pear and pistachios, and pheasant with truffle butter. To round out this marvelous list of stuffed pastas, try the veal-stuffed ravioli with tomato-basil sauce.

For seafood lovers there is a soup, a stew really, of shrimp, mussels, clams, oysters, and scallops in a rich tomato-saffron broth. Prego's menu is one that you can feel free to select anything that sounds good and the dish will be above your expectations in flavor and quality. Veal scallopini and saltimbocca, wood-grilled double lamb chops, Texas beef filet, and stuffed chicken breast will satisfy the most discerning meat-eaters. Save room for dessert, as the pastry chef offers a large selection to round out your meal.

Linguini with Littleneck Clams & Berkshire Pancetta

SERVES 4

Berkshire pork is considered some of the finest for the table. It is a heritage breed dating back 350 years to England. The meat is darker and the flavor much more pronounced than other commercial varieties. Kurabuta pork is from the Berkshire hog raised in Japan, but the name is also used in the United States to indicate the very highest quality of Berkshire pork one can use in the culinary arts.

½ cup diced yellow onion
¼ cup extra-virgin olive oil
8 ounces Berkshire pancetta (or other pancetta
    as available)
48 littleneck clams
8 ounces Frascati wine, or other Italian dry white
    wine (such as Trebbiano)
¼ cup chopped fresh oregano
Salt and freshly ground pepper
2 pounds cooked linguine (12 ounces dry pasta)

Sauté the onion in the olive oil with the pancetta in a large skillet until the onion is translucent and the pancetta has browned, about 6 minutes.

Add the clams and the wine. Toss briefly and cover. Cook 5 minutes over low heat or until the clams open. Discard any that remain closed.

Add the oregano and adjust seasoning with salt and pepper.

Toss in the cooked linguine and cook 1 minute to heat the pasta through. Divide the pasta among 4 bowls and add 12 clams to each. Serve immediately.

Quattro

Downtown
Four Seasons Hotel, 1300 Lamar Street
(713) 650-1300
www.fourseasons.com/houston/dining/quattro
Chef: Maurizio Ferrarese
Owner: Four Seasons Hotel

Nestled in the fourth floor of the Four Seasons Hotel, there is a polished, casual restaurant that operates as an independent restaurant would, and the food is so good it easily competes with them. Houstonians no longer think that you have to stay at a hotel to enjoy its restaurant's cuisine, and this is a trend among many of Houston's finer hotels. Chef Ferrarese sees to the exquisite preparations that distill the essence of the ingredients and makes them stand out and sing. His philosophy is simple—flavor. "Be true to your ingredients" is his credo. Chef Ferrarese has traveled the world, working in major cities to absorb the knowledge that led to his Michelin star in Prague as executive sous chef.

The asparagus risotto is asparagus first and rice second, vibrantly green from using copious amounts of the freshest asparagus to be found. The food is "straightforward Italian," but it is the straightforward Italian of Italy and not the traditional American interpretation. The fresh pea soup, redolent of freshly shucked peas, hides morsels of sweetbreads and earthy morel mushrooms. Delicate ravioli are filled with artichoke purée and topped with snail ragout. Elegant in its simplicity is the veal cutlet topped with arugula and cherry tomato salad, finished with Parmigiana Reggiano curls. If your mood is spaghetti and meatballs, try the paccheri (short, wide tubes similar to rigatoni) with delicate lamb meatballs and marinara. Quattro has an outstanding wine program—feel free to allow the knowledgeable sommelier to select the perfect glass or bottle to accompany your meal, or relax at the wine bar and enjoy a more casual evening.

SUMMER PEA SOUP
WITH MORELS & SWEETBREADS

SERVES 6

Organ meats have not been very popular among American diners, but should be. Sweetbreads have a delicate flavor and texture and complement other more bold flavors, such as wild mushrooms. One restaurant trick to firm up their texture is to press sweetbreads under weights overnight in the refrigerator.

2 shallots, peeled and sliced

½ cup extra-virgin olive oil

3 cups fresh shucked peas (or frozen, but not canned)

Boiling water

Salt and pepper

2 ounces dry morel mushrooms
   (or 12 ounces fresh, if in season)

2 tablespoons butter

2 tablespoons minced shallots

10 ounces sweetbreads, veins removed,
   soaked in milk 2 hours

2 peppercorns

1 bay leaf

Pinch of salt

1 tablespoon white vinegar

3 ounces ricotta cheese

Sauté the sliced shallots in 2 tablespoons of olive oil over medium heat. Add the peas and sauté 2 minutes.

Pour boiling water over the peas to cover and simmer 10 minutes, adding water as necessary. Strain the peas, reserving the simmering liquid.

Purée the peas with some of the simmering liquid in a blender, adding as much of the liquid as you can, but keeping the purée from getting too thin. You may be able to add all of the liquid.

With the blender running, add the remaining olive oil in a stream, forming a smooth creamy mixture. If still too thick, add some water. Strain through a fine sieve and reserve. Adjust seasoning with salt and pepper.

Soak dry morels in warm water for 1 hour and then rinse them thoroughly under running water to clean.

Heat the butter in a sauté pan over medium heat. Add the minced shallots and cook 1 minute. Halve the morels and add them to the pan. Sauté 5 minutes over low heat until tender.

Rinse the sweetbreads under running water 2 minutes.

Heat a pot of water to a boil with the peppercorns, bay leaf, salt, and vinegar. Add the sweetbreads and lower the heat to a simmer. Cook 3 minutes and remove the sweetbreads to an ice water bath. When cool, peel the skin from the sweetbreads and cut into ½-inch dice.

Add the sweetbreads to the morels in the sauté pan and briefly heat through. Adjust seasoning with salt and pepper.

Warm the pea soup over low heat. Form quenelles of ricotta and place them in the center of warm bowls. Add portions of morel-sweetbread mixture and pour soup over. Serve immediately.

RDG and Bar Annie

Galleria/Uptown
1800 Post Oak Boulevard
(713) 840-1111
www.rdgbarannie.com
Executive Chef: Robert Del Grande
Owner: Schiller-Del Grande Group

Robert Del Grande is an icon of modern Southwestern cuisine and one of its founding chefs. His latest venture, RDG, is the sequel to Cafe Annie, one of Houston's most famous restaurants. Cafe Annie had a profound influence on chefs and restaurants across the United States since the 1980s. Having had national exposure on television (*Great Chefs* with Pierre Franey and *Cooking with Master Chefs* with Julia Child from the

1990s), Robert has had to adapt to an amount of fame that can bring with it an assumption that he might be aloof and unapproachable. Nothing can be further from the truth.

Both the food at RDG and Robert Del Grande himself are friendly and approachable, in a true Texas way. His relaxed demeanor filters through to every dish. There are no elaborate garnishes to his exquisite recipes. Occasionally he throws a bit of humor into his plate presentations. Delicately smoked oysters, still plump and juicy, barely cooked, are bathed in barbecue sauce and served in a lidded, shiny metal can. Each dish is carefully thought out with regard to his clientele, and so the *chilequilles* that Texans grew up with for weekend Mexican breakfast form the bed on which a perfectly cooked red snapper fillet rests. Diced avocado and sharp Mexican cheese are the crown to this simple yet sophisticated dish.

When local, seasonal ingredients are at their peak, Robert jumps on the opportunity. Chilled fava bean soup, tart with citrus and bursting with perfectly cooked favas, is a fine example. While the kitchen crew complains about the tedious chore of hand shucking the beans, the end result is worth it many times over. Chef Del Grande reminds us, though, that not all things must be locally obtained to be enjoyed by Houston chefs and diners. He cites Texans' love affair with avocados in all forms; not one is grown within the borders of this vast state. Never "Tex-Mex," true Mexican influences appear throughout the menu, including a perfectly cooked steak topped with an intense mole from Oaxaca. Scattered across the plate can only be described as "debris," a term used by New Orleans cooks for the leftovers on the cutting board when slicing slowly roasted beef for sandwiches.

ROASTED QUAIL WITH PUMPKIN SEED SAUCE

SERVES 4

Pumpkin seed sauce is a sauce of the Yucatan peninsula and is considered a mole type of sauce. It is most often served with chicken in Mexico. Pumpkin or other squash seeds are first roasted to intensify flavor, and then are ground and mixed with fresh garlic, cumin, cilantro, and dried hot chiles.

3 ounces pumpkin seeds

2 ounces pine nuts

2 cups chicken stock

4 whole garlic cloves, peeled

¼ white onion, diced

2 poblano chiles, charred, skinned,
　　seeds and membrane removed

1 tablespoon fresh tarragon leaves

½ cup cilantro sprigs

2 tablespoons butter

1 teaspoon salt

8 boneless quail, wing tips removed

2 tablespoons extra-virgin olive oil

¼ cup crème fraîche or sour cream (optional)

Cilantro sprigs

In a dry skillet over medium heat, lightly toast the pumpkin seeds while constantly shaking until they begin to puff and pop, and then remove them from the pan. Be careful not to burn the seeds. Reserve approximately 1 ounce of the pumpkin seeds for garnish.

In a similar manner, toast the pine nuts until they are lightly golden.

Combine the chicken stock, garlic, and onion in a saucepan. Bring the chicken stock to a boil and lower the heat to a simmer. Cook the mixture over low heat for 15 to 20 minutes or until the onion and garlic are soft. Cool to room temperature.

Transfer the peeled chiles and the toasted nuts to a blender. Add the chicken stock with onion and garlic. Add the tarragon leaves and cilantro and purée until smooth.

Transfer the purée to a saucepan and bring to a simmer over low heat. Adjust the thickness if necessary with chicken stock or water. Stir in the butter and the salt. Reserve the sauce warm until needed.

Lightly rub the quail with olive oil and season with salt and pepper. Heat 2 tablespoons of olive oil in a wide skillet over medium-high heat. In batches so as not to overcrowd the skillet, brown the quail on all sides.

Transfer the browned quail to an ovenproof roasting pan. Roast the quail at 375°F for approximately 15 to 20 minutes or until the quail are just done.

To serve, spoon some pumpkin seed sauce on each dinner plate. Arrange the quail over the sauce. Drizzle some crème fraîche over each plate. Sprinkle the reserved pumpkin seeds over the quail. Garnish with cilantro sprigs and serve.

BBQ Oysters on Banana Leaves

SERVES 4 AS APPETIZER

Robert has also served these oysters in small metal cans for a unique presentation. For best flavor shuck oysters in shell rather than purchasing shucked oysters in a plastic tub.

12 ounces shucked raw oysters

1 cup water

½ tablespoon salt

½ cup extra-virgin olive oil

2 canned chipotle chiles in adobo, mashed or puréed

¼ cup adobo sauce from the canned chipotle chiles

1 tablespoon ketchup

2 tablespoons lime juice

Pinch of salt and pepper

6 pieces banana leaves, cut into 6-inch squares
    (corn husks may substitute—soaked to soften)

Coarse salt

Lime wedges

Brine the oysters overnight in the water and salt, covered and refrigerated. Drain and reserve refrigerated.

For the barbecue sauce, combine the olive oil, mashed chipotle chiles, adobo sauce, ketchup, lime juice, and salt and pepper.

Combine the oysters with about ¼ cup of barbecue sauce and toss to thoroughly coat the oysters.

Prepare a charcoal fire on an outdoor grill, with the coals to one side. When the coals are ready, place the banana leaf squares on the opposite side of the fire.

Divide the oysters among the banana leaves and add a few soaked wood chips to the fire to create some smoke. Close the grill and slowly smoke the oysters, about 30 minutes at 225°F. Check to see that the temperature is not too hot during smoking. The oysters should not brown or burn.

When done they should be firm and just release a bit of juice. Place the banana leaf squares on plates and drizzle the oysters with remaining barbecue sauce. Sprinkle with a touch of coarse salt and serve with lime wedges.

Samba Grille

Downtown
530 Texas Street
(713) 343-1180
www.sambagrillehouston.com
Chef: David Guerrero
Owners: Nathan Ketcham and Estella Erdmann

In the heart of Houston's theater district is Bayou Place, a complex of theaters, restaurants, clubs, and an aquarium. The Samba Grille is neatly nestled between other stylish restaurants and serves spectacular food for the theater crowd as well as all Houstonians seeking carefully prepared food made from the highest quality ingredients. The decor is modern and classy, yet welcoming, as is the staff.

Owner Nathan Ketcham describes the cuisine as Central and South American inspired (especially Brazilian, as his partner Estella Erdmann is from Brazil) with a dose of Texas thrown into the mix. This is not your typical churrascaria with gauchos dancing across the floor with swords of meat. There is rodizio, prix-fixe dinner with traditional skewered meats, but without the cliché. The service is impeccable and the menu is

creative and intelligent. Imagine succulent crab cakes delicately bound with yucca instead of expected bread crumbs, topped with passion fruit beurre blanc, or slowly roasted pork belly glazed with tamarind, so tender it shreds with the gentlest pressure from a fork.

BRAZILIAN CRAB CAKES WITH PASSION FRUIT BUTTER SAUCE

MAKES 8 (5-OUNCE) CRAB CAKES

Passion fruit is an aromatic fruit of a tropical vine that is native to Brazil. Its perfume-like aroma is like no other fruit and is used throughout the world, especially in desserts and beverages. Called *maracuyá* in Brazil, the name passion fruit came from Catholic missionaries who believed the three stigmas represented the hand wounds of Christ and the five anthers the five wounds.

For the crab cakes:

1 pound yucca, peeled, boiled, cooled, and grated
4 ounces scallions, finely chopped
1 teaspoon chopped Italian parsley
1 teaspoon crushed red pepper
2 tablespoons melted butter
1½ pounds jumbo lump crabmeat

For the passion fruit sauce:

¼ cup sliced shallots
2 tablespoons olive oil
4 roasted garlic cloves, puréed
8 ounces passion fruit pulp
¾ cup heavy cream
1 cup white wine
1 pound chilled butter, cut into cubes
Salt and pepper

Mix the grated yucca with the scallions, parsley, red pepper, and melted butter. Gently fold in the crabmeat and form into 8 cakes.

For the sauce, sauté the shallots in olive oil until soft. Add the garlic purée and cook about 1 minute. Add the passion fruit pulp and simmer for 5 minutes.

Add the cream, wine, and salt. Simmer for 5 minutes at medium heat.

Whisk in the butter, a few cubes at a time, off heat, until all of the butter has been added and the sauce has thickened. Adjust seasoning with salt and pepper.

Pour the sauce into a blender and pulse at low speed until smooth. Hold the sauce at 140°F until needed.

FARMERS' MARKETS

Urban Harvest is a nonprofit organization dedicated to educating the young and old (and everyone in between) about healthy foods that can be grown in the urban environment of Houston. In the 1980s the Interfaith Hunger Coalition proposed organic gardening as a potential solution to the hunger and nutrition issues of the urban poor, and in 1994 it became Urban Harvest with a much broader scope of educating the public of the benefits of nutritionally sound foods. In addition to education, Urban Harvest works hands-on to help neighborhoods and communities set up their own gardens and has helped to set up more than seventy-five school gardens. They offer classes, have a reference library, and can help with problems in existing gardens. They also oversee five farmers' markets in and around the city.

The City Hall Farmers Market runs on Wednesday at 901 Bagby, but is on winter break during the cold months. Sugarland opens its weekly market on Thursday, and Houston Community College (HCC) runs a market on Friday. The Saturday market, from 8 a.m. to noon, is on Richmond and is called the Eastside Market (the cross street is Eastside Street, just west of Kirby). Organic vegetables, meats, cheeses, flowers, arts and crafts, and food vendors all make this a busy and interesting venue for a Saturday morning. On Sunday morning the Highland Village market is open in the upscale shopping center, providing a local farmers' market to the River Oaks and Upper Kirby neighborhoods.

Many of the chefs who work in the restaurants of this book take advantage of locally grown organic produce and other foods, such as artisanal cheeses, heritage meats, local seafood, and fresh herbs, and support these urban markets. Several restaurants, including Hugo's and Backstreet Cafe, provide financial support as well, helping to ensure that Houston chefs have the best available ingredients to make superior dishes.

ETHNIC MARKETS

When you want to try a recipe from this book that calls for an ingredient that your local supermarket doesn't have (*aji amarillo* chiles for a recipe from Latin Bites Cafe as an example), where will you go? With the cultural diversity of a city like Houston, specialized markets to meet the needs of ethnic minorities abound. Houston has a large Asian population, and there are quite a few markets to enjoy hunting down that certain ingredient necessary to duplicate the dish enjoyed at a favorite restaurant. Ranch 99 Market in Memorial is a great place to start your shopping for all sorts of Asian foods—Korean, Japanese, Chinese, and Vietnamese. Part of a chain from California, it specializes in very fresh produce, high-quality meats, and a great bakery, unusual for an Asian market. Super H-Mart, also in Memorial, is mostly Korean in its fare and offers samples as you wander through the store. It's easy to find help, with many workers on the floor ready to assist you. The food court alone is worth the trip. The produce is fresh and crisp and the store is immaculately clean.

For exquisitely fresh fish to make sashimi plates or sushi at home, the Nippon Daido market in Westchase is the spot to go. This small Japanese market has an impressive selection of fresh and dried noodles and an assortment of sake that makes it difficult to pick just one.

When it comes to quality meats, think kosher or halal. Jews and Muslims have very similar high standards for the processing of meat, and halal markets often carry goat, which can be purchased in quarters or sides for that perfect *cabrito* roasting party. The Jerusalem Halal Meat Market is so much more than its name. It has a remarkable variety of olive oils, and the deli in the back has delicious food and a place to sit and dine. For such a small place, the selection of Middle Eastern goods is impressive. Because of the large Jewish population in Houston, two of the large supermarkets, Kroger's and Randall's, have kosher butcher shops in their stores in River Oaks with full-time rabbis to ensure authenticity and highest quality. Just outside the Loop, HEB Pantry Foods has a selection of prepackaged kosher meats. For olives, freshly baked pita, and terrific feta cheese, Droubi's Bakery and Imports is the place to go. While browsing the market, think about having a sandwich in the deli. The shawarma is exceptional. Phoenicia Specialty Foods is an important destination for Middle Eastern and Greek specialties. They bake all of their breads in-house and have a nice selection of cheeses, olives, and deli items such as hummus. Their baked goods are not to be missed, and their coffees from around the world are a fine complement to their pastries.

For South American delicacies try Gran Tangolandia for produce, canned goods, and yerba mate from Argentina, Peru, and Uruguay. Aji amarillo chiles and dried corn and potatoes from Peru may be difficult to find elsewhere.

For an incredible assortment of Latin American produce, canned goods, and meats, Fiesta Mart is the most convenient store to shop, with over twenty locations in Greater Houston. In addition to Latin American specialties, there are rows of international canned goods that you may not be able to find at any other market.

If you've tried to prepare Indian cuisine, you know the frustration of hunting down ingredients. India Grocers in Sharpstown solves this problem nicely. In addition to reasonably priced fresh spices, they have premixed spice packets for various Indian dishes and grains, lentils, and other pulses in bulk. Fresh herbs, such as curry leaf, can also be found in this large market at Hillcroft and 59.

Ethiopian cuisine is very spicy with unique seasoning blends, and the Maru Ethiopian Grocery is the place to go for your ingredients such as *t'eff* for making *injera* bread, although you should probably just purchase freshly prepared *injera* from them. Known for having some of the best coffee in the world, Maru offers four Ethiopian selections. If you don't want to cook, enjoy their delightful cafe and order a plate of *doro wat*, chicken in hot pepper sauce.

FOLK ART HOUSES

John and Mary Milkovisch have since passed away, but their legacy lives on, immortalized in beer cans. The Beer Can House at 222 Malone Street, between Memorial and Washington Avenue, has been a landmark of Houston for over thirty years, over which time John had flattened beer cans and sheathed his house with these recycled cylinders. In addition there are spirals of cut beer cans that twirl and sing in the wind and garlands of can tops strung together that hang like icicles year-round. John never considered himself a folk artist or new-age recycler.

"I guess I thought it was a good idea. And it's easier than painting" was John's take on it. Asked what his favorite beer was, considering there are well over 50,000 cans on the house, John simply replied, "Whatever's on special." Today it is under the care of the Orange Show Center for Visionary Art and is being lovingly restored with volunteer help and generous donations from the National Endowment for the Arts, Spaw-Maxwell, and others.

The Flower Man's folk art house is an island of beauty in the Third Ward of Houston, an area marked by rundown and abandoned buildings. Folk artist Cleveland Turner had a vision as he lay dying from alcohol poisoning—a homeless man who spent years living on the street and eating from church dumpsters and those of fried chicken fast-food establishments. He made a pact with God that, if he lived, he'd rent a condemned house and make it beautiful by raising lovely flowers, as he recalled his mom did when he was a boy. True to his word, he created gardens full of colorful flowers and cruised the neighborhoods to find discarded junk that he turned into art to display in his yard. Eventually he moved to 2305 Francis Street in the same neighborhood, taking along all of his yard art and flowers. He has expanded his work to vacant lots, one of which houses a dome made from bicycle rims encasing a Kwanzaa cow.

SHADE

THE HEIGHTS
250 WEST 19TH STREET
(713) 863-7500
WWW.SHADEHEIGHTS.COM
CHEF: GREGG BEEBE
OWNER: CLAIRE SMITH

The Heights is undergoing a renaissance. This eccentric and eclectic neighborhood is named for its elevation, twenty-three feet higher than Houston's fifty feet above sea level. It banned the sale of alcoholic beverages in 1912 and renewed the ban in 2000. As with most restaurants in the Heights, Shade gets around this by forming a private club for the consumption of alcoholic beverages, including the selections on their intelligent and thoughtful wine list. By ordering a drink and showing your ID, you instantly become a member.

Shade is supported by regulars and locals. Its decor is restrained and open, a place to eat without worrying about how to dress. The food is understandable and direct, and great care is placed as to what else is on the plate besides the fish, meat, or poultry. Their talented chef, Gregg Beebe, is responsible for this point of view, and he attributes his love of food to being raised on a farm. He understood quickly what fresh really means to a recipe's success.

The luscious halibut fillet rests atop a mélange of sweet pea gnocchi, lump crab, and sautéed baby shiitake mushrooms. Succulent Gulf shrimp, panko-coated and perfectly fried, are held up by a bed of bacon and cheese grits with a rim of Frank's RedHot sauce. Short ribs are surrounded by short rib "debris," a mixture of shreds of rib meat and bits of whatever falls from the bones when cooking.

Especially wonderful is the Thai-inspired curry that brings red snapper to life in a surprising way. Reminiscent of *kao soi*, a northern Thai specialty, red curry and coconut milk are simmered with pickled ginger, chiffonade of Napa cabbage, and crisp wonton slices. To accompany a lamb chop, a homemade lamb sausage is offered, juicy and spicy, with a snap to its skin.

Charcoal-Grilled Mustard-Marinated Leg of Lamb with Smoked Eggplant Sauce

SERVES 6

Globe eggplant are large and purple and come as male or female. The male is longer and narrow, while the female is more bulbous. Some feel the female is less bitter than the male. Feel free to substitute Japanese eggplant, which are light purple, narrow, and small, or round Thai eggplant that are mottled green and white, about the size of an egg.

For the leg of lamb:

6 ounces red wine

¼ cup Dijon mustard

¼ cup chopped mixed herbs such as Italian parsley,
    sage, and thyme

6 (6-ounce) lamb steaks cut from the leg

1 large globe eggplant, about 1½ pounds,
    cut lengthwise into quarters

Salt

1 shallot, finely diced

2 tablespoons oil

6 ounces soft goat cheese

3 cups chicken stock

Salt and pepper

For the stuffed Roma tomatoes:

6 Roma tomatoes, ends trimmed, seeds spooned out

8 ounces cooked couscous

2 tablespoons finely diced red onion

2 tablespoons finely diced red bell pepper

2 leaves fresh basil, chiffonade

2 tablespoons chopped oil-cured kalamata olives

Salt and pepper

1 cup dry unseasoned bread crumbs such as panko

Olive oil

For the roasted fennel bulbs:

2 large fennel bulbs, fronds removed,
    bases trimmed, each cut into 3 wedges

Juice and zest of 1 orange

1 cup dry white wine

2 tablespoons butter

Salt and pepper

Mix the red wine with the mustard and mixed herbs. Add the lamb steaks and thoroughly coat. Marinate at least 4 hours or overnight.

Place the eggplant on paper towels and salt all cut sides thoroughly. Allow them to stand 30 minutes. Pat them dry, removing any of the bitter brown liquid and most of the salt.

Build a charcoal fire, with the coals to one side. When ready, add some wet wood chips to the coals and place the eggplant on the side opposite of the coals. Cover and smoke the eggplant until very soft, about 30 minutes. Scrape the flesh of the eggplant from the skin and reserve.

Sauté the shallot in the oil. Add the smoked eggplant and goat cheese and whisk to combine. Add the chicken stock, whisking as it is added. Simmer 10 minutes. Place in a blender and pulse to form a uniform sauce. Adjust seasoning and reserve until needed.

Pat the lamb steaks dry and cook over hot coals to medium-rare or to desired doneness.

To prepare the tomatoes, mix the couscous with the red onion, bell pepper, basil, and chopped olives together. Adjust seasoning with salt and pepper.

Stuff each seeded Roma tomato with this mixture. Place the tomatoes on a sheet pan and top with bread crumbs. Drizzle olive oil over and place in a 350°F oven.

Roast the tomatoes for 20 minutes or until soft and the bread crumbs are golden.

For the roasted fennel, place the fennel wedges in a single layer into a large baking dish. Add the juice and zest of the orange, the white wine, butter, and salt and pepper.

Cover with foil and bake at 350°F for 30 minutes or until the bulbs are tender.

Serve the finished lamb steaks topped with any accumulated juices. Add some smoked eggplant sauce and a stuffed tomato and fennel bulb wedge to the side. Serve immediately.

HEIRLOOM TOMATO & GOAT CHEESE SALAD

SERVES 4

8 ounces goat cheese (chèvre) at room temperature
2 tablespoons heavy cream
1 cup basil
1 tablespoon toasted almonds
1 tablespoon Parmesan cheese
1 teaspoon garlic
Zest of 1 lemon
1 cup olive oil
1 cup kalamata olives
1 large shallot, diced
1 tablespoon capers
4–6 heirloom tomatoes cut into 16–24 slices
Coarse salt
Fresh ground pepper

Mix the goat cheese with the cream. Reserve this mixture.

Add the basil, almonds, Parmesan, garlic, and lemon zest to a processor or blender. While running, add ½ cup of the olive oil in a stream to form the pesto. Reserve.

Add the olives, shallot, and capers to a processor or blender. While the processor is running, add ¼ cup olive oil in a stream to form the tapenade. Reserve.

For each salad, place 4 to 6 slices of tomato on a chilled plate. Drizzle with goat cheese cream, 1 tablespoon pesto, 1 tablespoon tapenade, some coarse salt, a few twists of pepper, and a sprinkling of the remaining olive oil. Serve immediately.

Soma Sushi

Washington Avenue
4820 Washington Avenue
(713) 861-2726
www.somasushi.com
Sushi Chef: David Kim
Owner: The Azuma Group

Washington Avenue represents much of what the Houston dining scene is most recently about—young chefs willing to experiment, but within the confines of reason and sensibility. To describe the menu and style of food at Soma, one needs to think modern American meets Franco-Japanese. They engage the Japanese spirit of immaculately fresh ingredients, the thoughtfulness of exacting technique and exhaustive preparation of French cuisine, with the willingness to explore any culture or food to which America has been exposed. This is culinary diversity of the highest order.

Start with superior quality fish, and traditional sashimi and sushi are just a moment away from your table. Using the richest belly of salmon (*beni-toro*), on par with *o-toro* tuna, and the kitchen applies an Italian twist of *crudo,* with smoky olive oil, bold citrus, and apricot salt. Its Summer Ceviche is composed of *hamachi* and o-toro tuna with cilantro and pressed avocado, and comes as three mini-tacos, using taco shells made from egg roll wrapper. They stand upright on beds of sushi rice, a startling combination of Japanese and South American flavor. But fish is only one aspect of the menu's superlative offerings. The pork belly is cooked *sous vide,* slowly under vacuum and low temperature, to create fork-tender bites that mirror the flavor of the best *char sui* (Chinese red pork) you've had. Short ribs start with the finest American-raised Kobe beef and are done in the style of Korean *bulgogi,* and rest on small pools of soft goat cheese.

The meat is so tender that piercing a short rib cube with a fork only collapses it into a small pile of shredded beef. Sushi fans are rewarded with the Chef's Exotic Selections, including Icelandic Arctic char, Chinook ocean trout, East Coast fluke, and the difficult-to-obtain premium fatty o-toro bluefin tuna. Fans of tuna can also sample *hon maguro* (bluefin), *chu-toro* (medium fatty tuna), and Hawaiian big-eye tuna.

Miso Yum Soup

SERVES 8 AS MAIN DISH

This recipe is quite long and has many ingredients, preparation steps, and sub-recipes. Do as the professionals do in the restaurant kitchen and make the separate components at different times, well in advance of cooking and serving the dish.

For the chile paste:

¼ cup corn oil
½ cup chopped shallots
4 garlic cloves, minced
1 teaspoon chopped chile arbol
2 teaspoons chopped chile ancho
2 chiles pequin, crushed
2 Thai chiles, chopped
¼ teaspoon shrimp paste
1 allspice berry
½ teaspoon whole annatto seeds
½ teaspoon whole coriander seeds
1 teaspoon smoked paprika
½ teaspoon fresh thyme leaves
1 whole lime leaf

For the soup base:

4 quarts fish or chicken broth
1 teaspoon Goya azafran salt
1 tablespoon chopped fresh thyme leaves
2 teaspoons whole black peppercorns
2 whole cloves
2 lime leaves, chiffonade
1 (1-inch) piece galangal, peeled and sliced

16 large scallops (size U10)
24 fresh jumbo shrimp (size 16/20)
2 tablespoons peanut oil
24 black mussels, scrubbed, beards removed
1 cup lime juice
¼ cup fish sauce
1½ cups coconut milk
¼ cup red miso

2 cups chopped scallions
2 cups chopped cilantro, stems included
2 cups shredded Thai basil
1 pound cooked alimentary paste noodles
Hot chile oil

Add the corn oil to a large skillet over medium heat. Toss in the shallots and sauté, stirring often, 2 minutes.

When the shallots start to brown, add the garlic, turn down the heat, and sauté 2 minutes, being careful not to burn the shallots or garlic.

Stir in the chiles and shrimp paste and sauté briefly. Add the allspice, annatto, coriander, paprika, thyme, and lime leaf.

Remove from the heat and allow to steep, covered, 2 minutes. Using a blender or processor, pulse the mixture until a smooth paste forms. Reserve the paste until needed.

Measure ¼ cup of the reserved chile paste and stir it into the fish or chicken broth. Add the azafran, thyme, peppercorns, cloves, lime leaves, and galangal.

Heat to a simmer and immediately remove from the heat. Allow to steep 30 minutes. Strain and reserve the soup base.

Sear the scallops and shrimp over medium-high heat with the peanut oil in a wok or large skillet. Add the mussels and cook 2 minutes, stirring constantly.

To the reserved warm soup base, add the lime juice, fish sauce, and coconut milk. Stir in the red miso.

Divide the scallops, shrimp, mussels, scallions, cilantro, basil, and noodles among 8 large bowls. Ladle over the soup base. Drizzle chile oil over and serve immediately.

Sparrow Cookshop & Bar

Midtown
3701 Travis Street
(713) 524-6922
www.tafia.com
Chef/Owner: Monica Pope

Housed in a 1930s brick building in Midtown, Sparrow Cookshop & Bar (formerly t'afia) seems a perfect fit for the neighborhood location and its style. The seating and decor are casual and the emphasis is on the food. Monica Pope, owner and chef, has been working to master the balance of freshness, honesty of ingredients, and flavor for twenty years, and this is surely the culmination of her efforts.

In addition to the restaurant, Pope has generously given her time to hosting a farmers' market that has been meeting the needs of Houston's food-knowledgeable and chefs alike, as well as being one of the founders of the national movement of "farm to table." She is the only female chef to have won Top Ten New Chef from *Food and Wine* magazine. Her goal is to connect culture with food, to pair ingredients otherwise not anticipated to produce a unity of experience. Chef Pope wants to serve "fun food," honest food that is real and unprocessed. She is not one to jump on trends, but to believe in what she does. Her food is healthy and fresh, but with striking flavors.

A salad of endive, raw crimini mushrooms, blue cheese, crisp sweet pecans, and truffle dressing is a fine example of her understanding of how ingredients can reinforce and heighten each other. The truffle dressing is not used because truffles are a buzz word on many trendy menus. Rather flavorless raw mushrooms soar in their ability to react with their truffle cousin. Sweet Medjool dates are wrapped in salty bacon and chorizo, then finalized with *chermoula,* a North Africa seasoning that seems destined for this dish. Healthy grains are

seasoned to perfection and accompany dishes that play on their texture as well as flavor. Quinoa, the grain of life for the ancient Andean culture, pairs perfectly with the creamy texture of just-done scallops. The chewy texture of *colusari* red rice plays on the chewiness of Texas quail. An incredibly juicy, ripe Israeli melon is stuffed with crabmeat and dressed with Thai seasoning, making you want to bolt down the crab to settle in on the melon, which can be eaten right to the thin rind. Small plates such as chickpea fries with *sambal* ketchup, brown ale–battered crimini mushrooms with soy-ginger sauce, or a veggie plate of Yukon Gold potatoes, bacon, and maple syrup can make a meal for the senses and stomach alike.

Endive, Crimini & Blue Cheese Salad
SERVES 4

The Veldhuizen Family Farm produces world-class cheese. It is the epitome of small artisanal dairies, located just outside Dublin, Texas (home of the original Dr Pepper bottling company). To make this salad as special as can be, seek out Veldhuizen Bosque Blue, a Stilton-like cheese that is crumbly and drier than most. It is aged in separate caves on the farm for five to six months.

1 tablespoon whole grain mustard

2 tablespoons finely minced shallots

2 teaspoons chopped fresh thyme leaves

2 teaspoons coarse salt

¼ cup white balsamic vinegar

¾ cup grape seed oil

¼ cup white truffle oil

Salt and pepper

2 Belgian endives, white and red, halved, cut into ½-inch slices on the bias

8 small crimini mushrooms, cleaned, quartered

¼ cup Texas blue cheese, such as Bosque Blue from Veldhuizen Farms

½ cup toasted and chopped pecans

Coarse salt and white pepper

Mix the mustard, shallots, thyme, coarse salt, and balsamic vinegar in a blender. Slowly drizzle in the oils to form an emulsified dressing. Adjust seasoning with salt and pepper.

Add the sliced endives and crimini mushrooms to a bowl. Generously coat the salad with the dressing. Toss in the blue cheese and pecans.

Divide the salad among 4 chilled plates and sprinkle with coarse salt and pepper. Serve immediately.

BACON-WRAPPED CHORIZO-STUFFED MEDJOOL DATES WITH CHERMOULA

MAKES 16

Chermoula is a spice mixture from North Africa, where it is used as a marinade for fish and seafood, as well as for poultry meant for *tagine* cookery. It is also used as a salsa in Tunisia, with fiery chiles added.

For the stuffed dates:

16 large Medjool dates, opened (not cut through), pits removed
1 pound chorizo, casing removed, cooked, drained
8 slices smoked bacon, such as Nueske's Applewood, halved, cooked 50 percent

For the chermoula sauce (makes about 3 cups):

1 tablespoon minced garlic
1 bunch cilantro with stems, finely chopped
1 bunch Italian parsley with stems, finely chopped
1 cup Spanish paprika
2 tablespoons ground toasted cumin seeds
1 tablespoon cayenne
3 tablespoons salt
½ tablespoon fresh ground pepper
½ cup lime juice
1 cup olive oil

Overstuff each date with cooked chorizo, so the date almost cannot close.

Wrap a piece of bacon around each and place, seamside down, onto a baking tray.

Bake at 400°F for 5 to 7 minutes until the bacon is crisp and set around the dates.

To make chermoula, mix the garlic with the cilantro and parsley.

Mix the paprika with the cumin, cayenne, salt, and pepper. Add the spice mix to the herbs, mixing thoroughly.

Add the lime juice and beat in the oil. Serve the stuffed dates with the sauce on the side. The sauce stores well refrigerated.

Tasting Room

City Centre
818 Town and Country Boulevard
(281) 822-1500
www.tastingroomwines.com
Chef: Raymond Vandergaag
Owner: Lasko Enterprises

Imagine a clubby restaurant's wine tasting room. Then expand it to an entire restaurant. This is the impression as you walk in the door of the second Tasting Room, in City Centre, recently opened to serve corporate clients as well as regular diners (the original Tasting Room is on West Alabama near Kirby). Most tables and chairs are barstool height, perfect for gathering friends and standing around, sipping wine and noshing on a variety of tasty treats from the exposed kitchen and pizza oven. Racks and bottles of wine decorate the walls, and wooden cases are scattered around the perimeter. This is serious wine territory, brought to you by the group that gave Houston Max's Wine Dive. As with Max's, every wine can be purchased retail, as though you went to your local wine shop. With about 300 labels, there's quite a selection from which to choose.

Forty-eight wines are dispensed by the *enomatic* system, a nitrogen-charged automatic dispensing system that can measure a taste portion, half glass, or full glass.

You load a debit-like card with funds and swipe it at the dispenser to make your selections independent of the server. An additional twenty-six labels can be had by the glass, bypassing this high-tech system. In addition to tables there are three long bars placed strategically within the space, each with a view of the kitchen and specials board. Seating indoors is about 260, and there is space for another 300 on the expansive patio. Live music is offered regularly and wine tastings, paired with food, are scheduled every Saturday afternoon.

The menus pair well with the mission of enjoying wine. The cheese menu offers a dozen cheeses divided into categories of cow, goat, and sheep. There are seven *salumi* and cured meats, sliced to order, including prosciutto di Parma, Genoa salami, Spanish chorizo, and *coppa* (capicola). Pizzas are taken seriously as they make their own in-house mozzarella and use imported "OO" flour for the dough. Small bites such as duck confit sopas, *albondigas* (South American meatballs), brie and mushroom fondue, and oven-baked cheese with Mission figs, smoked bacon, and walnuts are perfect nibbles to enjoy with or without wine. Large plates include grilled corn ravioli, wood oven-roasted chicken, grilled flank steak, and cedar plank salmon. Their pastry chef entices you to have a dessert with Texas peach panna cotta, rich chocolate pudding (*budino*), and *zeppole* (ricotta doughnuts) on the dessert menu.

SHRIMP COCKTAIL IN SPICY TOMATO SAUCE

CAMPECHANA

SERVES 4

The shrimp cocktail served in the United States has the cocktail sauce separated from the shrimp. In this recipe, as done in Mexico, the shrimp are added to the sauce and allowed to marinate. A restaurant trick to perfectly cooked shrimp for a cocktail is to add the shrimp to boiling water, which will immediately stop boiling. As soon as the water returns to a boil, the shrimp are done and the pot is removed from the stove, the shrimp drained and immediately tossed into an ice-water bath to halt cooking. Cook the shrimp in shell for maximum flavor.

⅓ cup extra-virgin olive oil

½ cup ketchup

½ cup prepared chile sauce

2 tablespoons Tabasco

1 tablespoon chopped fresh oregano leaves

¼ cup chopped Italian parsley

1 tablespoon minced Serrano pepper, seeds and membrane left intact

1 tablespoon minced Fresno chile, seeds and membrane left intact

¼ cup lime juice

½ cup seeded and diced tomatoes

¼ cup diced red onion

1 teaspoon minced garlic

¼ cup chopped cilantro

½ teaspoon salt

1 pound jumbo shrimp (size 16/20)

3 lemons, cut in half

¼ cup Old Bay seasoning (or other seafood boil)

Diced avocado

Warm tortilla chips

Mix the oil with the ketchup, chile sauce, and Tabasco until the oil is absorbed.

Stir in the oregano, parsley, chiles, and lime juice.

Mix the tomatoes with the red onion, garlic, and cilantro. Add this to the chile sauce. Adjust seasoning with salt. Reserve refrigerated until needed.

Cook the shrimp in sufficient simmering water with the lemon halves and Old Bay seasoning until just done, about 3 minutes. Cool. Peel and devein. Cut each shrimp in half.

Add the shrimp to the reserved sauce and refrigerate 4 hours or overnight. Serve chilled in cocktail glasses garnished with diced avocado and a basket of warm tortilla chips.

III Forks

Downtown
1201 San Jacinto Street
(713) 658-9457
www.111forks.com
Chef: Ozzie Rogers
Owner: Consolidated Restaurant Operations

One of the few survivors in restaurant styles from the 1960s and '70s is the steak house. Americans love their beef and they enjoy large portions. Reasons that these restaurants are still successful include their ability to serve the finest prime beef not available to the general public and their high-temperature broilers that add greatly to the flavor. III Forks serves prime beef exclusively and cooks it to perfection. In addition their shellfish offerings are always popular, such as Australian lobster tails and gigantic shrimp. Salmon and Chilean sea bass round out the fish entrees.

The entrance to the dining rooms is striking with climate-controlled wine coolers, displaying an impressive array of labels, lining the walls. The atmosphere is warm and clubby, and the bar is inviting. As with most steak houses, the side dishes are a la carte. Unlike most, these are not an afterthought but are carefully and freshly prepared

vegetables. The deep-fried asparagus are perfectly cooked with a crisp breading and are then topped with a mountain of lump crabmeat. Mashed potatoes are garlicky, with diced green onion and some potato skin mixed in. Six-cheese scalloped potatoes are a meal in themselves. The creamed corn is the crown in this offering, cut right off the cob and seasoned with fresh thyme.

Don't miss the seafood medley appetizer with huge shrimp, bacon-wrapped sea scallop, a crab cake that is almost entirely crabmeat, and succulent calamari steak, sliced into strips and breaded. For carnivores try the croustades, slices of filet mignon on toast with mustard sauce. Salads are carefully prepared, and the house salad comes topped with generous blue cheese crumbles that are buttery and not too strong. For dessert a New Orleans–style bread pudding, rich and custardy, comes topped with a whiskey-caramel sauce loaded with native pecans and a scoop of cinnamon ice cream. You may need a "doggy bag" when you leave, and they are prepared for such a request.

OFF THE COB CREAMED CORN

SERVES 8

If you like your corn crunchy, reduce the steaming time to 5 minutes. Frozen kernel corn can substitute if fresh corn is not available.

8 ears corn, shucked and cleaned of silk

3 cups milk

3 cups heavy cream

2 tablespoons fresh thyme leaves

½ tablespoon fresh ground black pepper

1 teaspoon white pepper

½ tablespoon granulated garlic powder

½ tablespoon coarse salt

½ cup sugar

12 ounces (1½ cups) salted butter

½ cup flour

Steam the shucked corn on the cob for 10 minutes. Allow to cool.

Slice the kernels off the cob with a sharp knife. Reserve.

Heat the milk, cream, thyme, black and white peppers, garlic powder, salt, and sugar over medium-high heat in a large saucepan and bring to a simmer, stirring occasionally. Add the corn.

Melt the butter over low heat in a skillet. Whisk in the flour to form a smooth paste.

Cook the roux for 2 minutes, stirring occasionally.

When the corn mixture has reached 165°F, slowly add the roux while stirring.

Bring the mixture to a simmer. If the creamed corn is too thin, add up to 2 tablespoons more flour, whisking to incorporate. Serve immediately, or cool and store refrigerated.

TONY MANDOLA'S

RIVER OAKS
1212 WAUGH DRIVE
(713) 528-3474
WWW.TONYMANDOLAS.COM
EXECUTIVE CHEF: TONY MANDOLA
OWNERS: TONY AND PHYLLIS MANDOLA

Good things should happen to good people. Hard work should be rewarded. In spite of many cases where this doesn't seem to be true, it certainly is for Tony and Phyllis Mandola. Their success in Houston's restaurant scene is legendary. The Mandola family has been involved in food in this region for over 100 years, as farmers and ranchers, then butchers and market owners, and now as restaurateurs. Being the only daughter of Ninfa Laurenzo, Houston's icon of Tex-Mex cuisine, Phyllis seemed destined to carry on her parents' philosophy of satisfying customers and treating employees as family.

Recently Tony and Phyllis Mandola fulfilled a dream of owning their own place, and moved from a River Oaks mall location of over twenty years to become their own landlords. The problem was that the new restaurant would not be completed for several months after closing down the mall location, and their main concern was to keep their employees working. Coined the "miracle location," Tony arranged to take over a functioning restaurant space with an unheard-of short lease of a few months, just enough time to allow completion of Tony Mandola's and keep his employees gainfully employed.

In that time they were able to work on the new menu and hone their skills for opening the new spot. No matter how nice a location is, people dine out for the food, and this is the strongest link in the chain of Mandola's success. The food is delicious, attractively presented by highly trained and efficient staff, and orchestrated by Tony and Phyllis personally. The food is a tasty combination of "Mama's cooking," Creole and Cajun influences, and a bit of Italian tossed into the mix. Seafood is the main attraction, and the quality and care in which it is produced rivals the best of the Gulf Coast's seafood restaurants. Shrimp and Muenster-stuffed jalapeños are spicy and addictive, and to play on their Tex-Mex heritage, try the shrimp and crab quesadillas or the Cajun chalupas with juicy crawfish tails, avocado, and red beans for appetizers.

A traditional and correct gumbo is brimming with crab and shrimp, the roux is done just right, and the rich seafood stock is loaded with flavor. Red snapper is featured on the dinner menu, and they know how to cook it perfectly, whether topped with crawfish, broiled with rosemary in olive oil, or blackened and topped with crabmeat. New to the repertoire are their pizzas, and they are a success. Perfectly charred, the pizzas are topped with traditional Italian condiments, but the gumbo pizza is the surprising star of the show. To finish off a delightful dining experience, find room for banana-key lime pie. It will be worth the effort.

Mama Mandola's New Orleans Bread Puddin'

SERVES 12

There's no better way to use leftover, stale bread than to make a bread pudding. It is versatile and can include a variety of fruits, nuts, sweet spices, and liqueurs. It can be topped with custard sauce, caramel, or fruit purée.

For the bread pudding:

6 cups whole milk

¾ cup evaporated milk

4 eggs, beaten

1 pound melted unsalted butter

2 tablespoons vanilla extract

½ cup brandy

2½ baguettes dried French or Italian bread,
    cut into 1-inch slices

1¾ cups granulated sugar

2 tablespoons ground cinnamon

1 tablespoon freshly grated nutmeg

1½ cups golden raisins

3 Granny Smith apples, peeled, cored, and sliced

For the sauce Anglaise (makes about 2 cups):

1 cup whole milk

1 cup whipping cream

⅓ cup sugar

½ teaspoon vanilla extract

5 egg yolks

Preheat the oven to 300°F. Heat the milk with the evaporated milk in a heavy-bottomed saucepan. Carefully whisk in the eggs and melted butter. Stir in the vanilla and brandy.

Toss the bread with the sugar, cinnamon, and nutmeg in a large bowl. Add the milk mixture to soak the bread as much as possible. Add the raisins and apples. Allow the mixture to stand 5 minutes.

Place the mixture into a 10 x 12-inch casserole dish or baking pan. Cover with plastic film and then foil. Bake in a Bain Marie (a larger pan filled with water to come halfway up the sides of the casserole) in the preheated oven for about 45 minutes.

Remove the bread pudding from the oven and allow it to rest for 15 minutes.

While the pudding is cooling, make the sauce. In a heavy-bottomed medium saucepan bring the milk, cream, ¼ cup of the sugar, and the vanilla to a simmer. In an electric mixing bowl fitted with a whip attachment, beat the egg yolks and remaining sugar until pale.

Whisk some of the hot milk mixture into the egg mixture to temper and then add the tempered egg mixture to the milk mixture over a very low flame, stirring constantly. Cook until the mixture thickens and coats the back of a spoon. Do not allow the sauce to boil.

Remove from the heat and cover the surface with plastic film to prevent a skin from forming. Serve warm.

To serve, spoon or slice the bread pudding and place on dessert plates. Top with sauce Anglaise.

SNAPPER MARTHA

SERVES 6

Gulf red snapper is very popular in Houston restaurants for a good reason. It is a Gulf-caught fish that can be delivered at the peak of flavor and freshness, whose flesh is delicate yet rich in flavor, and is fairly unique to the region.

1 tablespoon coarse salt

½ teaspoon cracked black pepper

¼ teaspoon paprika

6 (8-ounce) skinless Gulf Coast snapper fillets

½ cup flour

¼ cup olive oil

12 jumbo shrimp (size 16/20), peeled and deveined

6 ounces peeled crawfish tails

6 ounces jumbo lump crabmeat

Salt

¼ cup seafood stock or fish broth (made from shrimp shells and snapper trimmings, if possible)

1 cup white wine

3 tablespoons chopped shallots

8 ounces (1 cup) cold unsalted butter, cut into pieces

3 tablespoons chopped basil

Combine the salt, pepper, and paprika. Dust both sides of the fish fillets with this mixture. Dredge the fillets in the flour.

Sauté the fillets in olive oil over medium heat in a large skillet. Cook about 2 minutes per side. Remove the fish from the pan to a plate, holding in a warm oven.

Add the shrimp to the skillet and cook about 1 minute or until the shrimp turn pink. Toss in the crawfish tails and jumbo lump crabmeat. Sauté the mix for 2 minutes, being careful not to break up the crabmeat. Add a pinch of salt. Remove the seafood from the skillet and keep warm in the oven.

Add the stock, white wine, and shallots to the skillet and reduce the volume by two-thirds over medium-high heat. Remove the pan from the heat and add the butter, 1 piece at a time, whisking or shaking the pan constantly. Add the basil.

Top each fillet with shrimp, crawfish, and crabmeat. Pour some butter sauce over and serve immediately.

BLACKENED CRAWFISH SALAD

SERVES 6

A Cajun technique of cooking meat or seafood with a dry rub over high heat to form a very dark crust is to blacken. The idea is not to burn the coating but to make it bold and highly aromatic, much like the roux used to thicken stews and such in Cajun cuisine.

For the crawfish:

2 pounds crawfish tails
4 ounces Cajun seasoning
3 ounces (6 tablespoons) melted butter

For the honey basil dressing (makes 1½ cups):

1 extra-large egg
1 tablespoon Creole mustard
¼ cup honey
1 cup olive oil
¼ teaspoon garlic powder
2 tablespoons white wine vinegar
1 tablespoon chopped fresh basil,
   leaves only
1 teaspoon coarse salt
1 teaspoon black pepper

For the salad:

1 pound spring mix lettuce
12 artichoke hearts, quartered
12 slices Roma tomatoes
6 thin slices red onion

Toss the crawfish tails with Cajun seasoning.

Add the melted butter to a hot skillet and then add the crawfish tails. Sauté over medium heat about 3 minutes, to "blacken."

To make the dressing, whisk the egg, mustard, and honey together in a mixing bowl.

Slowly add the oil while whisking constantly. Add 1 tablespoon hot water if needed to aid the emulsion.

Stir in the garlic powder, vinegar, basil, salt, and pepper. Refrigerate until needed.

Toss the spring salad mix with 1 cup honey basil dressing and portion equally onto 6 chilled salad plates.

Top the salads with equal portions of the blackened crawfish. Garnish with artichoke hearts, tomato, and red onion.

Tony's

Greenway Plaza
3755 Richmond Avenue
(713) 622-6778
www.tonyshouston.com
Chef: Grant Gordon
Owner: Tony Vallone

For almost fifty years Tony's has been the place to go for fine dining in Houston. To exist that long at the top requires a master at the helm, and Tony Vallone is that person. The formula for success seems to be a strict adherence to authenticity and quality of ingredients, with a careful eye toward modernization without trendiness. Tony's started in a space that the Galleria now rests upon, in 1965, and seven years ago he built his dream: a magnificent piece of architecture with an interior that is both sophisticated and inviting. Every interior detail has been addressed, from the control of noise to the broad spacing of tables to the decor. Service is impeccable and never obtrusive.

When Tony's menu states that all pasta is made by hand in house, realize that the flour is imported from Italy, the eggs are organic and free-range, and the water used

is bottled in Italy (yes, it does make a difference). The cheese-filled cappelletti (little hats) burst open when speared with a fork, onto the luscious vodka tomato cream sauce. Caviar crowns the little packages, offering a textural contrast along with a salty sea note. *Paglia e fieno* (straw and hay) are yellow and green tagliatelle in a delicate cream sauce, anointed with copious amounts of shaved truffles.

Your server first approaches with a bell jar covering burgundy truffles from Italy. These truffles are available only for a month or so in the early fall, before the white truffles of Umbria become available. The bell jar is lifted for you to savor the aroma. Tossing the warm pasta with the freshly shaved truffles releases their earthy perfume and readies your taste buds for a dining experience. Fish and seafood are featured and are carefully prepared and perfectly cooked. Soft-shell crab is paired with Gulf flounder in a white wine sauce. Branzino, or European sea bass, is simply dressed with garlic and olive oil,

sophistication in simplicity. There is Chilean sea bass, whole red snapper in salt crust, ahi tuna, Dover sole, and Atlantic salmon. For the beef connoisseur, forty-day natural-aged prime is hand-cut in house and is rich and fork-tender, with mineral overtones of properly aged beef.

I'm not sure it is possible to save room for dessert, but if you do, the *zeppole* (freshly fried doughnut holes filled with Nutella) can be popped into your mouth, or you can savor a fig tart with homemade vanilla bean ice cream. Cheesecake, tortes, and soufflé are also on menu to accompany a properly prepared espresso.

CRISP PORK PAILLARD WITH DIJON MUSTARD & CRIMINI MUSHROOMS

SERVES 4

Paillard refers to a cooking technique. Quickly sautéing pounded slices of meat was its definition that has been replaced over the years in France with the term *escalope*.

3 medium Idaho potatoes cut into ½-inch dice

½ cup olive oil, divided

1 loaf sourdough bread, crust removed

8 (3-ounce) slices pork loin, pounded with a mallet to ⅛-inch thickness

¼ cup Dijon mustard

1 tablespoon chopped fresh thyme leaves

8 ounces crimini mushrooms, sliced

1 teaspoon minced garlic

1 cup chicken stock

Salt and fresh ground pepper

½ teaspoon cornstarch

Sauté the potatoes in ¼ cup olive oil over medium heat. Cook until potatoes are done, about 8 minutes. Drain on paper towels and hold in a warm oven.

Cut the bread into pieces and place in a processor bowl. Pulse to form fine crumbs. Reserve.

Brush the pounded pork slices with mustard and sprinkle with thyme. Pat them in the bread crumbs, pressing to adhere the crumbs to the mustard coating.

Add the remaining ¼ cup olive oil to a large skillet and sauté the pork slices over medium heat until crisp, about 4 minutes on each side. Drain on paper towels and hold in a warm oven.

Add the mushrooms to the same pan. Add the garlic and sauté over medium heat about 3 minutes. Add the chicken stock and simmer 5 minutes. Season to taste with salt and pepper.

Dissolve the cornstarch in 3 tablespoons water and add it to the mushroom sauce. Bring the mixture to a boil to thicken.

Place 2 pork paillards on each plate and top with mushroom sauce. Scatter potatoes around and serve immediately.

Duck Lasagne with Taleggio

SERVES 8

The way professionals keep roasting duck from being too fatty is to pierce the skin all over with a metal skewer. Be careful not to pierce the flesh or juices will run out and the meat will be dry. Pull the skin away from the surface of the flesh as it is pierced.

1 cup diced carrots

1 cup diced celery

1 cup diced onions

12 fresh sage leaves, thinly sliced

¼ cup olive oil

2 ducks (3–4 pounds each), roasted, skin removed, meat pulled and shredded

4 cups demi-glace

Salt and pepper

3 tablespoons butter

½ tablespoon fresh thyme leaves

1 pound shiitake mushrooms, sliced

2 pounds cooked pasta sheets (about 12 ounces dry pasta), patted dry and rubbed with olive oil

1 pound Taleggio cheese, rind removed and sliced (freeze the cheese before slicing; it is soft)

4 cups béchamel sauce

Grated Parmesan

Sauté the carrots, celery, onions, and sage leaves in the olive oil in a large skillet over medium heat for about 6 minutes, or until vegetables are tender.

Add the duck meat and 2 cups of demi-glace to the vegetables. Stir and simmer 15 minutes over low heat. Remove from the pan and allow to cool. Season with salt and pepper.

Add the butter to the pan and sauté the thyme and mushrooms 3 minutes. Allow to cool. Season with salt and pepper.

Preheat the oven to 375°F. Coat a 10 x 15 x 3-inch lasagne pan with nonstick spray or a film of oil. Place a layer of pasta in the bottom of the pan. Add a thin layer of béchamel followed by a layer of half of the Taleggio cheese.

Add a second layer of pasta followed by béchamel and then half of the duck mixture.

Add another layer of pasta followed by béchamel and the mushrooms. Repeat with pasta, béchamel, and the remaining duck mixture. Add the remaining Taleggio cheese. Top with a final layer of pasta.

Spread some of the remaining demi-glace over the pasta and bake 1 hour 20 minutes in the preheated oven. When done, allow the lasagne to rest 20 minutes before cutting into 8 servings.

Top each portion with demi-glace and some Parmesan. Serve immediately.

Trevisio

Medical Center
6550 Bertner Street
(713) 749-0400
www.trevisiorestaurant.com
Chef: Jon Buchanan
Owners: Tracy Vaught and John Watt

The Texas Medical Center is one of the largest health facilities in the world and includes fourteen hospitals and three medical schools. It may be surprising to find a first-class restaurant among the various institutions, but Trevisio's mission is to serve the Texas Medical Center and to be an important amenity to the facility. The quality of food and service could easily make Trevisio a top ten stand-alone restaurant in any upscale neighborhood, and yet chooses to bless the doctors, nurses, students, visitors, patients, and their families with a superior dining experience. In addition the restaurant is constantly booked with catered events for 200 to 600 people, from medical conventions to weddings and bar mitzvahs.

Chef Jon Buchanan is at the helm, specializing in southern Italian dishes with a coastal Texas flair. The ingredients are the finest to be obtained, whether it is the brass die-cut pasta imported from Italy or the microgreens grown locally. Each dish is prepared with care and an attitude of "simple is best." Chef Buchanan learned well at Houston's most influential restaurant opened in the last fifty years—Cafe Annie, which began the modern food scene as it is known today. Under the tutelage of Robert Del Grande, Chef Buchanan learned to respect his ingredients and to allow them to speak without interference. His award-winning Lemon Risotto with Jumbo Lump Crab is spectacular and rich without being overbearing, using the finest imported Carnarolli rice. Be sure to ask for a spoon so as to not leave even one kernel of rice in the bowl. His custom-made wood-fired grill imparts subtle smokiness to octopus in an appetizer that includes house-cured pancetta and roasted fingerling potatoes. The steaks are dry aged in-house, and all of the breads and desserts are homemade on premises.

LEMON RISOTTO WITH JUMBO LUMP CRAB

SERVES 8

For the risotto:

¼ cup minced shallots
1 tablespoon minced garlic
¼ cup extra-virgin olive oil
2 cups Arborio rice, uncooked
2 cups white wine
Juice of 2 lemons
Zest of 1 lemon
6 cups hot chicken stock
½ cup heavy cream
½ cup grated *grana padano*
Salt and pepper

For the crab topping:

1 shallot, minced
1 garlic clove, minced
1 tablespoon extra-virgin olive oil
½ cup white wine
1 teaspoon black peppercorns
2 bay leaves
½ cup heavy cream
6 ounces (¾ cup) cold butter, cut into small pieces
Juice of 1 lemon
Salt and pepper
1 pound jumbo lump crabmeat, picked over
    for bits of shell and cartilage
Micro-basil for garnish

In a heavy, nonreactive pot, sauté the shallots and garlic in olive oil until translucent. Add the rice and continue to sauté until the rice develops a nutty aroma.

Deglaze the pan with white wine and juice of 2 lemons. Stir the rice with a rubber spatula or wooden spoon only, so as to not break up the rice while stirring. Continue stirring until the wine is almost all absorbed. Add the lemon zest.

Add ¼ cup hot chicken stock while constantly stirring. When the stock is almost absorbed, add an additional ¼ cup stock. When almost absorbed repeat this process until the rice is cooked, the stock has been used up, and a creamy texture has developed.

Stir in the heavy cream and grated cheese. Adjust seasoning with salt and pepper. Reserve warm.

In a nonreactive saucepan, sauté the shallot and garlic in olive oil over low heat until soft. Add the white wine, peppercorns, and bay leaves and simmer until reduced by half. Add the heavy cream and simmer until reduced by half.

Whisk in butter off heat, a few pieces at a time, until all the butter has been used. Add the juice of 1 lemon and adjust seasoning with salt and pepper.

Strain the sauce to remove the solids and add it to a clean saucepan. Add the jumbo lump crabmeat and slowly warm the crab in the sauce over low heat.

Add portions of risotto to warm bowls and top with crab and sauce. Garnish with micro-basil.

Uchi

Montrose
904 Westheimer Road
(713) 522-4808
www.uchirestaurants.com
Chef: Kaz Edwards
Owner: Tyson Cole

In the space formerly occupied by Felix Mexican Restaurant, James Beard award–winning Chef Tyson Cole (Best Chef: Southwest, 2010) of Austin Uchi fame, along with his Bravo *Top Chef* winner Paul Qui, opened Uchi in Houston, a perfect location for his talents to be appreciated. The original Uchi, which means "home" in Japanese, is a perfect name for their Houston location as well. This Montrose restaurant is homey more than formal in its service, a number one priority when the staff translated their Austin location into a Houston venue.

Chef Cole understands that the success of a restaurant is focused on the guest, and whatever they serve must be what the guest wants and expects. The food here is focused as well, relying on exquisitely fresh ingredients, whether locally grown or flown in daily from halfway around the world. Chef Cole insists that his style of food is not Japanese fusion, but relies on the tenets of authentic Japanese cuisine. To use a locally grown, in-season vegetable not eaten in Japan, but treated in the Japanese fashion, is not fusion cooking, according to Cole. Each dish served is constantly under scrutiny to evaluate its flavor profile and to see if it can be made better in some way. Nothing leaves the kitchen without being tasted and examined. Recipes are checked to see if anything unnecessary is being used that may interfere with the essence of what the main ingredient is all about. They strive for "the perfect bite" every time.

The menu is divided into categories such as Cool Tastings with yellowtail and Thai chile and orange segments as a tasty example. The fish is extraordinarily fresh and luscious, and the sauce a perfect complement with just the right amount of acidity. Under Hot Tastings the pork jowl with brussels sprouts is as unctuous a dish as can be had. The meat literally melts in your mouth and coats it with goodness. Some of the best fried chicken can be found at Uchi, with a crunchy and sweetly caramelized coating that begs to be licked off your fingers (rather than being wiped off with the courteous moist towel provided). To explore the menu in depth and the talents of the chef, go for the Omakase tasting menu of ten courses selected by Chef Cole. You will not be disappointed.

Uchi Fried Chicken

Karaage

SERVES 4

This is some of the best fried chicken you'll ever have. While there are multiple sub-recipes, plan early in the week and have them ready before the day you want to make the chicken. The sweet chile sauce and fish caramel would be nice to have in the refrigerator to add dimension to a variety of dishes, such as fish and pork.

For the sweet chile sauce (makes 8 cups):

3½ cups fish sauce
3½ cups white vinegar
¾ cup water
2 teaspoons salt
1¾ pounds sugar
7 ounces Korean chile flakes
12 ounces minced garlic
12 ounces sliced scallions, white parts only

For the chicken:

2 boneless chicken breasts, halved
2 cups sweet chile sauce (see above)
4 chicken wing drumettes
4 chicken wings
4 boneless thighs
½ cup sweet chile sauce (see above)
½ cup fish caramel (see below)
Cornstarch for dredging
Peanut oil for frying

For the fish caramel (makes about 6 cups):

3 ounces lemongrass, sliced thin
6 ounces minced garlic
4 ounces chopped shallots
2 medium onions, diced
Lard for frying
2 tablespoons minced Thai chiles
1 small bunch cilantro, chopped

1 sprig mint, chopped
2 tablespoons sherry vinegar
3 quarts water
8 pounds sugar
2 cups fish sauce

For the sweet chile sauce, combine the fish sauce, vinegar, and water. Mix the salt with the sugar and chili flakes. Combine the two mixtures. Stir in the garlic and scallions, mixing well. Refrigerate until needed.

Toss the chicken pieces with 2 cups sweet chile sauce and place into a resealable plastic bag. Allow to marinate 4 hours or overnight.

Dredge the chicken pieces in cornstarch and fry at 325°F until golden brown, about 6 minutes.

To make the fish caramel, sauté the lemongrass, garlic, shallots, and onions in lard over low heat in a large stockpot until the contents are caramelized and deeply golden in color, about 10 minutes.

Add the chiles, cilantro, and mint and slowly cook to dryness. Add the sherry vinegar and stir to deglaze the pan.

Add the water and sugar and cook over medium heat to reduce to one-fourth the volume. The mixture should coat the back of a spoon.

Add the fish sauce and continue to reduce to a syrup, coating the back of a spoon. Allow to cool and refrigerate until needed.

Toss the fried chicken with ½ cup sweet chile sauce mixed with ½ cup fish caramel. Cut the breasts and thighs into strips and serve immediately.

PORK JOWL WITH KIMCHI BRUSSELS SPROUTS

SERVES 6

Pork jowls are another of the cuts of pork that were very cheap and often the focus of poor people's dinner plates. They do require a lot of cooking time to make them tender, but braising in the oven is an easy way to do this. Today's chef would cook them *sous vide*, under vacuum in a bag resting in a water bath just above the final serving temperature of the meat, for several hours.

2 tablespoons unsalted butter
2 pounds pork jowl, cleaned, skin removed
1 teaspoon cinnamon, pan-toasted until aromatic
Salt and pepper
1½ cups minced shallots
4 Thai chiles, sliced thin
2 green onions, sliced
¼ cup minced garlic
¼ cup grated ginger
2 tablespoons Korean crushed red pepper
1 cup vegetable oil
½ cup white vinegar
3 tablespoons white soy
¼ cup fish sauce
1 pound brussels sprouts, quartered
Oil for frying
Fish Caramel (see previous recipe)

Heat the butter in a skillet over medium heat until it browns. Sauté the jowl briefly. Add the cinnamon and toss to coat. Remove from the heat. Season with salt and pepper.

Place the jowl in a vacuum bag and vacuum seal. Place in a pot of simmering water (180°F) for 5 hours, adding water as necessary.

While the jowl is cooking, prepare the kimchi base by sautéing the shallots, chiles, green onions, garlic, ginger, and crushed pepper in oil over low heat until a dry, red paste develops.

Mix the vinegar, soy, and fish sauce together and add to the chile paste. Cook over low heat until almost all liquid has evaporated.

Deep-fry the Brussels sprouts in 375°F oil until golden and crisp outside. Toss with the kimchi base and allow to stand at room temperature until the jowl is done.

Cut the jowl into 6-ounce slices and glaze with fish caramel over a grill, turning several times while basting.

Cut the pork jowl portions into pieces and place on top of a bed of Brussels sprouts. Serve immediately.

PIZZATOLA'S
1703 Shepherd Drive

The secret to the flavor of true Texas barbecue comes from the apparatus/method of cooking, and Pizzatola's has the only authentic barbecue pit remaining in Houston. Basically the pit is a long brick box (the pit) to contain the wood topped with grills to hold the meat; an arrangement of hinged lids opens and closes over the cooking meats, using counterweights. A typical pit may run eight to twenty feet in length. It takes quite a bit of skill to run a Texas barbecue pit, and there is usually a "pit boss," who is the equivalent of the head chef.

A Houston city ordinance no longer allows these pits in any city restaurant; Pizzatola's is "grandfathered" as it has been in operation since 1935, making it one of the oldest continually run restaurants in all of Houston. If it were to make any improvements to its building, it would have to

remove the pits, which would end the ability of Pizzatola's to produce the most authentic barbecue outside the Hill Country of Central Texas (the barbecue capital of the world).

In addition to great pork ribs, which are extremely tender yet not falling off the bone, having a perfect crust, smoke ring, and dry rub, Pizzatola's makes terrific sausage, using a loose packing of a fine grind of meat with just the right spice mix. The brisket has a balanced, meaty flavor that is not overpowered by smoke, but has a rich smokiness to complement the beef. The sauce is first rate, striking a balance between sweetness, sharp vinegar, and spiciness.

Eating barbecue is a messy business, and many places offer rolls of paper towels to help. Pizzatola's offers thick linen napkins—unheard of in barbecue restaurants—and finishes your dining experience with a moist, folded linen napkin.

BURN'S BARBECUE
7117 North Shepherd Drive

The ladies at Burn's are there to make your barbecue experience as good as it gets. In addition to being friendly and efficient (it gets really busy during lunch time), they cook up some of the best 'cue in town. They strike a delicate balance between flavor and smoke. *Delicate* is not usually a description of barbecue, but the smokiness is just right to complement the flavor of the meat being served.

The ribs are juicy without being fatty and have great flavor. The sausage is particularly good due to the medium grind of the filling, loose packing and ample seasoning, and a bit of heat on the finish. The brisket is lean with a good smoke ring, and the sauce, while thin, is smoky and goes well with the beef. Side dishes can make or break a barbecue dinner, and their chile beans are exceptional, with a surprise sweetness not often found at most places. You will not leave hungry, as their plates are loaded. The 3-Meat Lunch has generous portions of pork ribs, sausage, and brisket, along with two sides, bread, pickles, and onions—it can barely be lifted to carry to your table. They are set up for catering any number, so consider them an excellent choice for a large party.

VIRGIE'S BAR-B-QUE
5535 North Gessner Drive

A bit out of the way, Virgie's is worth the extra miles up Gessner. You are greeted with a big smile from the owner and a straightforward menu of barbecue standards. What separates Virgie's from everyone else, besides technique, is their sauce, which can make the experience of eating 'cue. Many sauces are too vinegary, but Virgie's is just right—enough to cut the richness without dominating the palate. It is sweet, but not cloyingly so, and has no tomato or mustard, but a molasses base. The meats are exceptionally prepared, and the ribs may be some of the best to be had in the state. The ribs are juicy but not fatty and very meaty with the taste of roasted pork; the meat gently pulls from the bone. The brisket is similarly juicy and meaty without being greasy.

THELMA'S BAR-B-CUE
3755 Southmore Boulevard at Scott Street

Thelma does it her way or no way. You have two choices for sauce, none or over your meats. You may not have it on the side. Do not tap on the window for service or you'll get none. If this sounds like a *Seinfeld* episode, you are not far off, but people flock to Thelma's for her "Eastside" barbecue nonetheless. Her notoriety began in 2002 when PBS featured her in a piece on "Sandwiches You Will Like" (her brisket sandwich). She has been written up in *Texas Monthly* and in Steve Raichlen's book about regional American barbecue, highlighting that personality and character can get you noticed. The original Thelma's burned down in 2009, a common fate for many barbecue restaurants, considering that open flames, wood, and grease make a volatile combination in an enclosed area.

As a side note on how enterprising Americans can be, just after it burned down, to accommodate a steady stream of barbecue seekers looking for a Thelma's lunch, a neighbor set up his small barbecue grill and started selling from his front yard.

Thelma's is home-style Southern cooking, and the side dishes are worth the trip to her new location on Scott. Especially good is the stewed okra and tomatoes. You will be warned that this is not fried okra, which many barbecue places serve when okra is on the side dish menu. The yams, redolent with honey, are also outstanding. In addition to the standard offerings, Thelma's features her version of what may be unique to Houston's barbecue scene, the stuffed baked potato: a split-open baked potato loaded with chopped barbecue or a selection of meats, in her 2-Meat Baked Potato.

Homemade pies and cakes are a great way to finish your meal, so be sure to ask what she's serving for dessert. Whole pies and cakes are available upon request.

GATLIN'S BBQ AND CATERING
1221½ West 19th

Right down the street from Hubcap's new location in the Heights is the bustling storefront of Gatlin's BBQ. Its main business has been catering large events, which it does effortlessly. In this small location for table dining, the service can be slow, so plan on some extra time for lunch and to find a place to park. The wait seems worth it once the food arrives, though. The ribs are meaty and lean, but not dry. They are tender with a good smoke ring and a fine bark. The brisket is just as good, with a great smoke flavor without being overbearing. The sausage has a nice grind to it, with a crisp, snappy skin and plenty of spicy heat. Sides are excellent, especially the dirty rice. The grains are separate and well seasoned, and the mix is rich in meaty bits. The baked beans are more of the New England style, but they also offer ranch-style beans for the traditionalist. Try the peach cobbler or bread pudding for dessert, if you have room.

EL HILDAGUENSE
6917 Long Point

Internet media and reviews will direct you to El Hildaguense for their Mexican barbecue, known as *barbacoa* (from which we get the term barbecue). Quickly it becomes evident that this is the best *barbacoa* in the city and so much more—one of the very best Mexican restaurants, period. They specialize in lamb and goat, and the lamb broth served with the lamb tacos is magnificent, with a surprise of chickpeas and rice resting on the bottom of the bowl. They have a huge, built-in kettle to simmer lamb stock continuously, tossing in bones and liquid as needed throughout the day. The tortillas and all *masa* products, such as gorditos, are hand-made to order. Rather than chips and salsa when you are seated, you'll be served a plate with chicken flautas accompanied by a unique hot sauce, one made exclusively from dried arbol and chipotle chiles. The tacos and gorditos are piled high with fillings such as pork with *nopales* (cactus), chicken in red mole, or slices of roasted lamb. As a final treat each guest is given a small plate of rice pudding to finish the meal. For large parties an entire roasted lamb (*borrega*) can feed forty and whole goats (*cabrito*) a dozen guests.

NAM GANG
1411 A Gessner

Outside the Loop in an unassuming strip center, Nam Gang serves up terrific Korean barbecue. The meats are of highest quality and, when cooked over glowing coals, define what this style of food is all about. If you want the experience of grilling beef short ribs yourself, the center of each table is a charcoal grill and above each table is a commercial grade exhaust hood. Different grilling plates are used for different meats, and the staff is friendly and willing to help with your grilling technique. If this seems like too much work, the kitchen will be glad to do the grilling in the back.

The *banchan*, little plates of marinated vegetables and other side dishes, are first rate. Eight different dishes accompany your meal—kimchee, marinated cucumbers, bean sprouts, spinach, seasoned potatoes, firm tofu, green beans, and mixed vegetable medley. Some are spicy, some tangy and fermented, and all complement the rich meats from the grill. The place is cozy, with each table separated from the other with high screens. Feel free to ask about any menu item. You will get an honest opinion from the friendly staff.

VALENTINO'S

GALLERIA
2525 WEST LOOP SOUTH
(713) 850-9200
WWW.VALENTINORESTAURANTGROUP.COM/VALENTINOHOUSTON
CHEF: CUNINGHAMME WEST
OWNERS: PIERO SELVAGGIO AND LUCIANO PELLIGRINI

The Hotel Derek is lucky to have one of Houston's most experienced chefs at the helm of Valentino's. Positioned diagonally across from the Galleria, this restaurant is popular among residents as well as travelers. The restaurant design is modern Italian, with reds and blacks subdued by the romantic lighting. The menu is modern Northern Italian, and Chef Cuninghamme West understands how to bring out flavors best by limiting the offerings on a plate. No need for dabs of multiple sauces and garnishes when a drizzle of superior olive oil and a few crunchy grains of sea salt will do.

Crudo is a perfect venue to display this philosophy. Defined as "raw" in Italian, Crudo on Valentino's menu offers the freshest raw fish, minimally dressed. Think Italian sashimi. Chef West creates a plate sampler with at least three varieties of fish, complemented with the finest Sicilian olive oil, sea salt crystals, and just a dab of flavored aioli. One of his signature treats is an ovenless pizza, cooked to perfection on the broiler. The crust is remarkably thin, crunchy, and a bit charred. Toppings are kept simple, such as pizza topped with thin slices of prosciutto and fresh arugula.

All pastas are handmade, and the lobster ravioli (Mezzaluna d'Aragosta), encased in striped pasta made from alternating strips of squid ink pasta and regular pasta, is ethereal and should not be missed. Seafood lovers will savor the crab cakes done Italian style, Scottish salmon with puttanesca sauce, or the seared scallops with lemon caper sauce. For the carnivore, consider a rack of lamb with orange gremolata, a veal chop with demi-glace, or the buttery New York strip perfectly grilled and served sliced with a drizzle of balsamic emulsion and arugula salad. A cheese plate is the perfect ending to a meal at Valentino's, and be sure to ask Chef West to include a dab of luxurious truffle honey to the condiments.

Caper Crêpe with Scallop & Chive Butter

SERVES 4

For the crepes:

¼ cup drained capers
Olive oil
1 cup flour
2 eggs
¾ cup whole milk
¼ cup water
2 tablespoons melted butter
Salt and pepper

2 tablespoons olive oil
1 tablespoon unsalted butter
8 jumbo scallops (size U10)
4 ounces (¼ cup) salted butter, room temperature
¼ cup chopped chives

For the sun-dried tomato sauce:

2 garlic cloves, minced
1 tablespoon olive oil
2 tablespoons minced yellow onion
½ cup chopped oil-packed sun-dried tomatoes
½ cup roughly chopped stewed tomatoes, with juice
2 large basil leaves
Salt and pepper
2 tablespoons butter

To serve:

Extra-virgin olive oil

To make the crepes, add the capers to a small saucepan and just cover with olive oil. Fry until the capers are crisp. Drain them and place on paper towels to remove excess oil.

Mix the flour and eggs together until smooth. Slowly whisk in the milk and water. Add the butter and pinch of salt and pepper.

In nonstick pan add enough of the batter to cover the bottom of the pan and sprinkle about 8 fried capers onto the batter before it is cooked. Tilt the pan to evenly cover the bottom. Cook 1 minute or until the surface seems dry and flip over to finish. Remove from pan and repeat the process until all of the batter is used. Reserve.

Heat 2 tablespoons of olive oil and the butter over high heat in a skillet. When the butter begins to brown, add the scallops, searing on each side 1 minute. The scallops should be rare.

Beat the softened butter with the chives. Add a dollop of chive butter to the center of each of 8 crêpes. Top with a scallop and fold over twice to form a quarter-circle.

Place the filled crêpes, covered in foil, into a 375°F oven for 6 to 8 minutes.

For the tomato sauce, lightly brown the garlic in the olive oil in a skillet. Add the onion and cook until translucent without browning, about 3 minutes.

Add the sun-dried tomatoes and stewed tomatoes with juice and simmer over low heat for 10 minutes, adding juice or water as needed.

Add the basil leaves and salt and pepper to taste. Remove from heat and allow to stand 5 minutes.

Add the tomato mixture to a blender and add the butter. Pulse to form a smooth sauce.

To each warmed plate add some sun-dried tomato sauce. Add 2 crêpes, overlapping, and drizzle with extra-virgin olive oil.

LOBSTER MEZZALUNE

SERVES 4

To add color to your pasta, replace some of the eggs with beet juice or spinach juice. Consider making two colors of pasta, cutting them into strips and rolling the strips together to make striped pasta.

For the filling:

2 lobster tails, about 5 ounces each, shells removed,
    tail meat sliced into medallions
2 tablespoons extra-virgin olive oil
1 large shallot, minced
1 tablespoon puréed roasted garlic
2 sprigs fresh thyme
¼ cup brandy
⅓ cup mascarpone
Salt and pepper

For the pasta:

2 cups flour
1 cup beaten eggs (about 3)

For the marinara sauce:

4 cloves garlic, thinly sliced
2 tablespoons olive oil
½ medium yellow onion, sliced
1½ cups roughly chopped stewed
    peeled tomatoes with juice
5 large basil leaves
Salt and pepper

To serve:

1 shallot, minced
2 garlic cloves, minced
Olive oil
Splash of vodka
Pinch of dried chile flakes
3 tablespoons butter
Sprig fresh thyme

4 (5-ounce) lobster tails, shells removed,
    tail meat sliced into medallions
Salt and pepper

For the filling, sauté the lobster meat in the olive oil with the shallots, roasted garlic, and the thyme, in a skillet over medium heat. Cook until the lobster meat is just cooked, about 2 minutes.

Deglaze the skillet with the brandy and remove from the heat. Allow to cool.

Transfer the contents of the skillet to a food processor and blend with the mascarpone cheese to form a smooth paste. Season with salt and pepper. Reserve refrigerated.

To make the pasta, place the flour in a large bowl and make a well in the center. Add the eggs to the well. Bring in the flour, a little at a time, until all the flour is incorporated. Knead by hand 5 minutes or until smooth and elastic. Wrap in plastic film and allow to rest 15 minutes.

Roll out the dough with a pasta machine. Cut 12 (3-inch) circles.

Place some of the lobster filling in the center of each circle. Moisten the edge with water and fold over to form a half-circle or half-moon. Remove any trapped air as you seal each tightly.

For the sauce lightly brown the sliced garlic in olive oil. Add the onion and sauté over medium heat until translucent. Add the tomatoes and simmer 20 minutes over low heat.

Add the basil leaves and remove from heat. Cover and allow to steep 10 minutes. Purée the tomato sauce in a blender or processor until smooth. Adjust seasoning with salt and pepper. Reserve the marinara sauce for service.

Add the pasta to lightly salted, simmering water, being careful not to break up the pasta with vigorously boiling water. Cook about 8 minutes. Drain on paper towels and keep warm in a holding oven.

Sauté the shallot and garlic in olive oil. Deglaze the pan with the vodka. Cook until most of the liquid has evaporated. Add the reserved marinara sauce and chile flakes.

Heat the butter and thyme in a separate saucepan over medium heat. When the mixture is hot, add the lobster medallions. Reduce the heat to low and sauté until cooked, about 2 minutes.

To serve, spread some marinara sauce on the bottom of large dinner plates. Bathe the cooked pasta mezzalune in the lobster-butter-thyme sauce and season with salt and pepper. Add the pasta to the plate and top with lobster medallions. Drizzle with the thyme butter. Serve immediately.

ZIMM'S LITTLE DECK

MONTROSE
601 RICHMOND AVENUE
(713) 527-8328
WWW.ZIMMSLITTLEDECK.COM
CHEF: FRANCIS LECRIQUE
OWNER: STEVE ZIMMERMAN

Restaurateur Steve Zimmerman was raised in New Orleans and to satisfy his craving for great Creole and Cajun food, he opened Zimm's Little Deck shortly before the remodel of La Colombe d'Or into CINQ. The Little Deck is on the eastern edge of Montrose, almost in Midtown, and is one of those neighborhood places that people bicycle and walk to, in order to feast on Creole comfort food. The place is cozy and narrow, and the long, broad marble bar, running half its length, welcomes you to not only enjoy a New Orleans cocktail but also to sit and have a meal.

The mac-and-cheese starter is ideal comfort food, and they got it just right. Not too saucy or dripping with melting cheese, this version has the flavor built into and surrounding the noodles, and the crust is crunchy but not too thick. The fried green tomatoes are just right—firm and tart without being sour and under-ripe. The menu rotates often—if you

are lucky enough to see the fried pig's ears on the menu, jump on the opportunity. Sandwiches include Poor Boys and Rich Boys. Poor Boys are filled with fried oysters, shrimp, and/or crawfish. Roast beef and what the menu calls "boring" chicken are also available. Rich Boys have sautéed beef tips, duck confit, spicy *merguez* sausages, or pulled pork and are enhanced with caramelized onions, cherry glaze, Asian slaw, or red wine/shallot reduction.

When the weather is nice, consider settling into a game of *petanque* on their adjacent manicured court. Petanque is similar to Italian bocce. Metal balls are lobbed as close to a wooden jack as possible, a bit like playing horseshoes. Competition can get feverish, so brush up on the rules and practice during slow periods to avoid beginner's anxiety. Their small, paved deck outside is perfect for watching a match or just dining alfresco.

CHICKEN, SAUSAGE & SHRIMP GUMBO

SERVES 4

A restaurant secret to making a dark roux without standing over it, constantly stirring, for at least 30 minutes, is to mix the flour with the oil and place it in a heavy skillet in a 325°F oven to slowly brown without stirring. Large quantities can be made in this way to have on hand.

1 (3-pound) chicken

4 sprigs fresh thyme

3 bay leaves

2 pounds shrimp, peeled and deveined (save shells for stock)

2 cups bottled clam juice

3 tablespoons black peppercorns

8 ounces (1 cup) butter

¾ cup all-purpose flour

½ chopped yellow onion

¼ cup chopped green bell pepper

2 garlic cloves, minced

¼ cup chopped celery

1 cup sliced fresh okra

1 tablespoon gumbo/creole seasoning (such as Paul Prudhomme or Tony Chachares)

1 teaspoon dried thyme

1 teaspoon dried basil

½ teaspoon finely ground black pepper

Tabasco sauce to taste

1½ cups smoked sausage, sliced diagonally

1 cup chopped canned tomatoes with juice

Salt and pepper

1 pound raw jasmine rice, cooked and reserved for serving

1 cup chopped scallions

Place the chicken in a pot and cover with water. Add the thyme sprigs, bay leaves, shrimp shells (saved from cleaning the shrimp), clam juice, and peppercorns. Cook over low heat for 45 minutes. Remove the chicken and allow to cool.

Strain the stock through a fine-mesh strainer and return it to the stove. Reduce the stock by half.

Once chicken has cooled completely, remove the skin and pull the meat from the bones. Discard the bones.

Melt the butter in a large saucepan over low heat. Add the flour and cook, stirring often, 30 to 45 minutes until the roux has become dark brown in color.

Add the chopped onion, bell pepper, garlic, and celery. Sauté the vegetables in the roux until tender. Add the okra and cook 5 minutes.

Stir in the gumbo seasoning, thyme, basil, and black pepper. Add Tabasco to taste.

Add the smoked sausage, shrimp, reserved chicken, and tomatoes. Simmer 1 hour or until thickened. Adjust seasoning with salt, pepper, and additional Tabasco sauce.

Serve over cooked rice and top with chopped scallions.

Fried Green Tomatoes with Creamy Herb Dressing

SERVES 4

While always a staple of Southern cooking, this dish became popular after the similarly titled movie was released in 1991, starring Jessica Tandy. Green tomatoes are unripe red tomatoes (rather than tomatillos, which are green when ripe) and are utilized in recipes like this at the end of the growing season, when there are still some green tomatoes on the vine that will not have time to ripen.

For the dressing:

¼ cup dry parsley flakes
1 teaspoon black pepper
2 tablespoons onion salt
1 teaspoon garlic salt
1 teaspoon salt
2 tablespoons MSG (optional)
1 quart mayonnaise
1 pint sour cream
1 pint buttermilk

For the tomatoes:

2 quarts peanut oil
6 eggs, beaten
1 tablespoon Tabasco sauce
2 cups yellow cornmeal
2 cups flour
2 tablespoons salt
2 tablespoons pepper
4 pounds green tomatoes,
    cored and sliced thick

Mix the dry ingredients together for the dressing. Mix the mayonnaise, sour cream, and buttermilk together. Combine the 2 mixtures and allow to stand, refrigerated, 4 hours or overnight. (Prepared ranch dressing may substitute for this dressing.)

Heat the oil to 350°F.

Whisk the eggs with the Tabasco sauce.

Mix the cornmeal, flour, salt, and pepper together.

Dip the tomato slices in the egg wash and then evenly coat in the cornmeal mixture.

Fry, in batches, until golden brown, about 3 minutes per side. Drain on paper towels.

Drizzle the dressing over the fried tomatoes and serve immediately.

Recipe Index

Almond Pear Tart with Brown Butter Ice Cream, 27–28
Asparagus & Beet Salad, 21–22
avocados
    Avocado Relish, 37
    Crabmeat Cocktail, 61

banana leaves, BBQ oysters on, 136–37
basil, in Pesto, 73
beef
    about: where chefs eat hamburgers, 68–71
    Beef & Pork Meatballs in Spicy Broth with Vegetables, 62–63
    Beef Croustades, 66–67
    Garlic Beef, 91
    Shaking Beef with Chile Lime Vinaigrette, 48
    Slow-Braised Short Ribs, 100–101
    Smoked Pepper Steak, 7
beets, in Asparagus & Beet Salad, 21–22
bread pudding, 159
Biscuits & Andouille Sausage Gravy, Country-Fried Chicken Livers, 53
brussels sprouts, pork jowl with, 171

cheese
    Cream Cheese Frosting, 114–15
    Endive, Crimini & Blue Cheese Salad, 151
    Heirloom Tomato & Goat Cheese Salad, 146
    Max 'n Cheese, 96–97
    Piquillo Peppers Stuffed with Local Goat Cheese & Porcini, 74–75
    Warm Goat Cheese & Potato Salad, 124
chicken
    Chicken, Sausage & Shrimp Gumbo, 181
    Chicken Vindaloo with Turmeric Rice, 128–29
    Country-Fried Chicken Livers on Biscuits & Gravy, 53
    Cream of Poblano Soup with Roasted Corn & Sausage, 103–4
    Lemon Garlic Chicken with Butternut Squash, 88–89

Rigatoncini with Pesto, Fregola, Roasted Chicken & Portobellos, 73
Smoked Chicken & Potato Hash with Poached Eggs, 4
Uchi Fried Chicken, 170–71
citrus
    Chile Lime Vinaigrette, 48
    Lemon Risotto with Jumbo Lump Crab, 167–68
corn and polenta
    Cream of Poblano Soup with Roasted Corn & Sausage, 103–4
    Off the Cob Creamed Corn, 157
    Peruvian Sashimi with Three Sauces, 84–85
    Seared Swordfish with Mushroom Ragout on Truffled Polenta, 58–59
    Texas Cobb Salad, 6
crêpes, caper, with scallop & chive butter, 177

dates, bacon-wrapped chorizo-stuffed Medjool, with chermoula, 152
desserts
    Almond Pear Tart with Brown Butter Ice Cream, 27–28
    Brown Butter Ice Cream, 29
    Cream Cheese Frosting, 114–15
    Hummingbird Cake, 114–15
    Mama Mandola's New Orleans Bread Puddin', 159
    Sticky Toffee Pudding with Toffee Sauce, 19
    Tea Cake with Marinated Strawberries, 12–13
Duck Lasagne with Taleggio, 164–65
dumplings
    about: where chefs eat, 49–50
    Steamed Shrimp & Crab Dumplings, 46–47

eggplant, in Smoked Eggplant Sauce, 145–46
eggs
    Crème Brulée French Toast, 98
    Smoked Chicken & Potato Hash with Poached Eggs, 4
    Spaghetti alla Carbonara, 40–41

Endive, Crimini & Blue Cheese Salad, 151

fennel
    Roasted Fennel Bulbs, 145–46
    Seared Diver Scallops with Roasted Fennel Purée, 23
fish and seafood
    BBQ Oysters on Banana Leaves, 136–37
    Blackened Crawfish Salad, 161
    Brazilian Crab Cakes with Passion Fruit Butter Sauce, 139
    Caper Crêpe with Scallop & Chive Butter, 177
    Chicken, Sausage & Shrimp Gumbo, 181
    Citrus-Marinated Fresh Cod Fillet with Coriander Potato Salad, 16
    Crabmeat Cocktail, 61
    Crispy Rice Paper Salmon, 125
    Eel Sauce, 80
    Fish Caramel, 170
    Fried Oysters, 122
    Grilled Salmon with Wheat Berries & Lentils, 29–30
    Grouper with Jalapeño Grits & Avocado Relish, 36–37
    Gulf Flounder en Brodo, 32–33
    Gulf Shrimp Corn Dogs with Tabasco Mash Remoulade, 54–55
    Lemon Risotto with Jumbo Lump Crab, 167–68
    Linguine alla Gamberoni, 39–40
    Linguini with Littleneck Clams & Berkshire Pancetta, 131
    Lobster Mezzalune, 178–79
    Miso Yum Soup, 148–49
    Ouisie's Splendid Spud, 121
    Peruvian Sashimi with Three Sauces, 84–85
    Pescado a Lo Macho, 83
    Provençal Mussels, 15
    Red Snapper Sashimi with Pickled Grapes, 9
    Sashimi Tuna & Soba Noodles with Jicama Slaw, 94–95
    Scallop & Foie Gras Sushi, 80–81
    Seafood Mulligatawny Soup, 76–77

Seared Diver Scallops with Roasted
    Fennel Purée, 23
Seared Swordfish with Mushroom
    Ragout on Truffled Polenta,
    58–59
Shrimp Cocktail in Spicy Tomato
    Sauce, 155
Snapper D'Amico, 44
Snapper Martha, 160
Snapper Nino, 109
Steamed Shrimp & Crab
    Dumplings, 46–47
foie gras
    Foie Gras Torchon, 13
    Scallop & Foie Gras Sushi, 80–81
French toast, crème brulée, 98

garlic, black, 40
green beans, Hunan, 48
gumbo, chicken, sausage &
    shrimp, 181

Honey Basil Dressing, 161

ice cream. See desserts

Jicama Slaw, 94–95

lamb, Charcoal-Grilled Mustard-
    Marinated Leg of Lamb with
    Smoked Eggplant Sauce, 145–46
lentils, in Grilled Salmon with Wheat
    Berries & Lentils, 29–30
liver
    Country-Fried Chicken Livers on
        Biscuits & Gravy, 53
    Foie Gras Torchon, 13
    Scallop & Foie Gras Sushi, 80–81

Miso Yum Soup, 148–49
mushrooms
    Crisp Pork Paillard with Dijon
        Mustard & Crimini
        Mushrooms, 163
    Endive, Crimini & Blue Cheese
        Salad, 151
    Marinated Pork Tenderloin with
        Pan-Roasted Mushrooms, 87
    Rigatoncini with Pesto, Fregola,
        Roasted Chicken &
        Portobellos, 73

Seared Swordfish with Mushroom
    Ragout on Truffled Polenta,
    58–59

onions, pickled, 117–18
oysters. See fish and seafood

Passion Fruit Butter Sauce, 139
pasta
    Duck Lasagne with Taleggio,
        164–65
    Linguine alla Gamberoni, 39–40
    Linguini with Littleneck Clams &
        Berkshire Pancetta, 131
    Lobster Mezzalune, 178–79
    Max 'n Cheese, 96–97
    Rigatoncini with Pesto, Fregola,
        Roasted Chicken &
        Portobellos, 73
    Sashimi Tuna & Soba Noodles with
        Jicama Slaw, 94–95
    Spaghetti alla Carbonara, 40–41
pears
    Almond Pear Tart with Brown
        Butter Ice Cream, 27–28
    Stuffed Poached Pear Salad with
        Blue Cheese, Dried Fruits &
        Nuts, 2–3
peas
    Field Pea Salad, 23
    Summer Pea Soup with Morsels &
        Sweetbreads, 133
peppers
    Cream of Poblano Soup with
        Roasted Corn & Sausage,
        103–4
    Piquillo Peppers Stuffed with Local
        Goat Cheese & Porcini, 74–75
    Red Pepper & Roasted Tomato
        Gazpacho, 106
pork
    Andouille Sausage Gravy, 53
    Bacon-Wrapped Chorizo-Stuffed
        Dates with Chermoula, 152
    Beef & Pork Meatballs in Spicy
        Broth with Vegetables, 62–63
    Chicken, Sausage & Shrimp
        Gumbo, 181
    Cream of Poblano Soup with
        Roasted Corn & Sausage,
        103–4

Crisp Pork Paillard with
    Dijon Mustard & Crimini
    Mushrooms, 163
"Kakuni" Braised Pork Belly, 79
Linguini with Littleneck Clams &
    Berkshire Pancetta, 131
Marinated Pork Tenderloin with
    Pan-Roasted Mushrooms, 87
Pork Jowl with Kimchi Brussels
    Sprouts, 171
Pork Roast Yucatan Style,
    117–18
7-Spice Braised Pork Shanks,
    56–57
potatoes
    Coriander Potato Salad, 16
    Ouisie's Splendid Spud, 121
    Smoked Chicken & Potato Hash
        with Poached Eggs, 4
    Veal Schnitzel, 106–7
    Warm Goat Cheese & Potato
        Salad, 124
Pumpkin Seed Sauce, 135

quail, roasted with pumpkin seed
    sauce, 135

rice
    about: rice papers/wrappers, 125
    Chicken, Sausage & Shrimp
        Gumbo, 181
    Chicken Vindaloo with Turmeric
        Rice, 128–29
    Crispy Rice Paper Salmon, 125
    Lemon Risotto with Jumbo Lump
        Crab, 167–68
    Pescado a Lo Macho, 83
    Risotto, 57

salads
    Asparagus & Beet Salad, 21–22
    Blackened Crawfish Salad, 161
    Coriander Potato Salad, 16
    Endive, Crimini & Blue Cheese
        Salad, 151
    Field Pea Salad, 23
    Heirloom Tomato & Goat Cheese
        Salad, 146
    Heirloom Yellow Tomato &
        Watermelon Salad, 35
    Jicama Slaw, 94–95

Stuffed Poached Pear Salad with
Blue Cheese, Dried Fruits &
Nuts, 2–3
Texas Cobb Salad, 6
Warm Goat Cheese & Potato
Salad, 124
sauces and condiments
Andouille Sausage Gravy, 53
Avocado Relish, 37
Chermoula Sauce, 152
Chile Lime Vinaigrette, 48
Chile Paste, 148
Citrus-Herb Yogurt, 22
Creamy Herb Dressing, 182
Eel Sauce, 80
Fish Caramel, 170
Honey Basil Dressing, 161
Marinara Sauce, 178–79
Mushroom Ragout, 58–59
Passion Fruit Butter Sauce, 139
Pesto, 73
Pumpkin Seed Sauce, 135
Red Sauce (for oysters), 122
Sun-Dried Tomato Sauce, 177
Sweet Chile Sauce, 170
Tabasco Mash Remoulade, 54–55
Tagliarini Pomodoro, 32
Vinaigrette, 16, 22

sauces (sweet) and frostings
Cream Cheese Frosting, 114–15
Sauce Anglaise, 159
Toffee Sauce, 19
seafood. See fish and seafood
soups, stews, and stocks
Beef & Pork Meatballs in Spicy
Broth with Vegetables, 62–63
Cream of Poblano Soup with
Roasted Corn & Sausage,
103–4
Miso Yum Soup, 148–49
Red Pepper & Roasted Tomato
Gazpacho, 106
Seafood Mulligatawny Soup, 76–77
Summer Pea Soup with Morsels &
Sweetbreads, 133
squash
Lemon Garlic Chicken with
Butternut Squash, 88–89
Squash Medley, 125
strawberries, in Tea Cake with
Marinated Strawberries, 12–13
sushi, foie gras & scallop, 80–81

tofu, firm, with tomato, 65
tomatoes
Firm Tofu with Tomato, 65

Fried Green Tomatoes with Creamy
Herb Dressing, 182–83
Heirloom Tomato & Goat Cheese
Salad, 146
Heirloom Yellow Tomato &
Watermelon Salad, 35
Marinara Sauce, 178–79
Red Pepper & Roasted Tomato
Gazpacho, 106
Stuffed Roma Tomatoes, 145–46
Sun-Dried Tomato Sauce, 177
Tagliarini Pomodoro, 32

veal
Veal Piccata, 41
Veal Schnitzel, 106–7
Veal Vincent, 110
vinaigrettes. See sauces and
condiments

watermelon
Crabmeat Cocktail, 61
Heirloom Yellow Tomato &
Watermelon Salad, 35
wheat berries, in Grilled Salmon with
Wheat Berries & Lentils, 29–30

General Index

Asia Market, 51
Asian, where chefs eat, 49–51
Azuma Group, The, 78, 147

Backstreet Cafe, 1–4
Banana Leaf, 50–51
barbecue, where chefs eat, 172–75
Barbed Rose, 5–7
Barry's Pizza and Italian Diner, 25
Beck's Prime, 70
Beebe, Gregg, 144
benjy's Upper Washington, 8–9
Bernie's Burger Bus, 71
Bistro Alex, 10–13
Bistro Provence, 14–17

Branch Water Tavern, 18–19
Brasserie 19, 20–23
Brooks, Elizabeth, 26
Brother's Pizza, 25
Buchanan, Jon, 166
Bui, Van, 64
Burn's Barbecue, 173
Butera, Joe, 38

Canopy, 26–30
Castre, Roberto, 82
Chaney, Jason, 5
Ciao Bello, 31–33
Cinq, 34–37
Clark, Charles, 20, 72

Cole, Tyson, 169
Consolidated Restaurant
Operations, 156
Cox, Mark, 92

Damian's Cucina Italiana, 38–41
D'Amico, Nash, 42
D'Amico's Italian Market Cafe, 42–44
Dang, Anny, 64
Del Grande, Robert, 134
Dolce Vita, 24

Edwards, Kaz, 169
El Hildaguense, 175
Erdmann, Estella, 138

ethnic markets, 142–43
Evans, Randy, 52

farmers' markets, 140
Ferrarese, Maurizio, 132
folk art houses, 143
food festivals, 111
Four Seasons Hotel, 132
Fung's Kitchen, 51

Gatlin's BBQ and Catering, 174
Gigi's Asian Bistro and Dumpling Bar, 45–48
Gordon, Grant, 162
Grappino di Nino, 108–10
Greek festivals, 111
Grossman, David, 18–19
Guerrero, David, 138

hamburgers, where chefs eat, 68–71
Haven, 52–55
Hong Kong Dim Sum, 49–50
Horiuchi, Manabu, 78
Hotel Sorella, 10
Huang, Gigi, 45
Hubbell and Hudson Bistro, 56–59
Hubcap Grill, 70–71
Hugo's, 60–63
Huynh, 64–67

Ibiza Food and Wine Bar, 72–75
ICON (hotel), 86
Indika, 76–77
Italian festival, 111

Jaisinghani, Anita, 76, 127
Jaisinghani, Ravi, 76
Jones, Elouise Adams, 120

Kata Robata, 78–81
Ketcham, Nathan, 138
Khun Kay, 49
Kim, David, 147

Lankford's Cafe, 69
Lasco Enterprises, 96, 153
Latin Bites Cafe, 82–85
Lecrique, Francis, 34–35, 180
Legacy Restaurants, 116

Levit, Benjy, 8
Line and Lariat, 86–89
Luna, David, 86

Mai's Restaurant, 90–91
Mandola, Frankie, 38
Mandola, Tony and Phyllis, 158
Mandola, Vincent, 108
markets, 140–43
Mark's American Cuisine, 92–95
Marriot Hotel Group, 86
Matos, Bobby, 31
Max's Wine Dive, 96–98
McGraw, Amanda, 20
McKissack, Jeff, 126
Milkovisch, John and Mary, 143
Mockingbird Bistro, 99–101
Molina family, 102
Molina's Cantina, 102–4
Monarch, 105–7

Nam Gang, 175
Nguyen, Mai, 90
Nino's, 108–10

O'Donnell, Vanessa, 113
Ooh La La Dessert Boutique, 113–15
Orange Show, 126
Original Ninfa's on Navigation, 116–19
Ortega, Hugo, 1, 60
Ouisie's Table, 120–22

Padilla, Alex, 116
Palacios, Napoleon, 38
Pat and Joe's Bellaire Broiler Burger, 69
Pellegrino, Michael, 96
Pelligrini, Luciano, 176
Pham, Anna, 90
Philippe, Jean and Genevieve, 14
Philippe Restaurant and Lounge, 123–25
pizza, where chefs eat, 24–25
Pizzatola's, 172–73
Pondicheri, 127–29
Pope, Monica, 150
Potowski, Mike, 8
Prego, 130–31

Quattro, 132–33

Ramos, Carlos, 82
RDG and Bar Annie, 134–37
Rogers, Ozzie, 156
Romano's Italian Restaurant, 24

Saigon Padolac, 50
Samba Grill, 138–39
Schiller-Del Grande Group, 134
Schmit, Philippe, 123–24
Selvaggio, Piero, 176
Shade, 144–46
Sheely, John, 99
Simmons, Austin, 56
Smith, Claire, 26, 144
Soma Sushi, 147–49
Soza, Rolando, 10
Sparkle's Chill Spot, 68
Sparrow Cookshop & Bar, 150–52
Star Pizza, 24–25
street cars, 61

Tasting Room, 153–55
Thai festivals, 111
Thelma's Bar-B-Cue, 174
III Forks, 156–57
Tony Mandola's, 158–61
Tony's, 162–65
Trevisio, 166–68

Uchi, 169–71

Valentino's, 176–79
Vallone, Tony, 31, 162
Vandergaag, Raymond, 153
Vaught, Tracy, 1, 60, 166
Vincent's, 108–10
Virgie's Bar-B-Que, 173

Watt, John, 130, 166
West, Adam, 105
West, Cuninghamme, 176

Z Resorts, 105
Zimmerman, Steve, 34–35, 180
Zimm's Little Deck, 180–83

About the Author

Arthur L. Meyer is a restaurant and bakery consultant who has cooked professionally since 1963. He has taught cooking internationally, is considered an expert on world cuisines, and has achieved Master status in baking. He opened a specialty bakery in 1983, which became the subject and name of his first cookbook, *Texas Tortes* (1997). *Texas Tortes* has recently been re-released in paperback. Art has written three additional cookbooks, including *Baking Across America* (1998), and he coauthored *The Appetizer Atlas* (2003), which won Best Foreign Language Cookbook–English and Best in the World from Gourmand Cookbook Awards in 2003. *The Appetizer Atlas* has been his bestseller and has become a mainstay in many professional kitchens. Its popularity can be attributed to its detailed research on the cuisines of the world and the popularity of appetizers and small bites with home cooks and chefs alike. Art's fourth book, *Corsican Cuisine*, was published in 2010, and his fifth cookbook, *Danish Cooking and Baking Traditions*, was released in spring 2011. Art resides in Austin, Texas, where he was a lecturer in organic chemistry for fourteen years at the University of Texas and where he continues to teach chemistry at the community college.